Collection
of Selected CaoDai Holy Messages

Translated by Hum D. Bui, MD. and Hong D. Bui, M.D.
Edited by Ngasha Beck-Huy

CreateSpace
2015

ISBN-13: 978-1517564117

Copyright Hum D. Bui, MD and Hong D. Bui, MD

CONTENTS BOOK 1

18 - Foreword of the Sacerdotal Council

19 – Introduction of Janet Alison Hoskins, Professor of USC

21 – Forward of the translator

24 - Christmas 1925 The Jade Emperor introduces Himself and announce the names of the first twelve disciples.

25 - Jan 3, 1926 Spiritism and Automatic Writing.

27 - Feb 20, 1926 Unity, Cooperation and the Glorifying of the Way. From now on, the Master begins teaching the Way.

30 – Feb 23, 1926 To teach children

31 - Feb 25, 1926 The rites and the veneration of the Divine Eye.

34 - Mar 13, 1926 The truth and the falsehood . . . Remember that I have sent many wild beasts to surround you and to bite you every day; but do not worry, because I have already given you an armor for your protection.

35 – April 7, 1926 The Master is also Nhien Dang Co Phat, Thich Ca Mau Ni, Thai Thuong Nguon Thi

36 - April 8, 1926 Sakyamuni Buddha is happy for the coming of the Way and Duc Cao Dai explains the meaning of "Tam Ky Pho Do."

38 - April 22-23, 1926 Organizing the heavenly appointments and the oaths.

41 - April 24, 1926 The Creation of the Five Branches of the Great Way and the Master does not leave the dharma in human hands.

42 - April 26, 1926 The first heavenly appointment.

43 - May 30, 1926 Saving all beings, even the unborn; the previous incarnation for the creation of Buddhism. The founding of CaoDai is by miraculous spiritism but not by re-incarnation.

45 - May 31, 1926 The divine heart and the human heart. Advice to adepts to save humanity.

46 - June 5, 1926 Sakyamuni Buddha comes to save living beings under the name Cao Dai Tien Ong Dai Bo Tat Ma Ha Tat...

48 - June 8, 1926 Teaching in French for Two French Guests attending a Séance.

50 - June 27, 1926 Rituals.

53 - July 5, 1926 Advice for dignitary K.

54 - July 15,19 26 Establishment of the cenacle "Ngoc Dan".

55 - July 17, 1926 Establishment of the College of Women.

56 - July 17, 1926 Miraculous dharma and cultivation by meditation.

58 - July 22, 1926 The death and eternal life. God says: "If I did not exist, there would be nothing in the universe. And if there were no Cosmic Ether, then I would not exist either."

60 - July 25, 1926 Self-cultivation.

61 - July 30, 1926 Divine teaching regarding adultery.

63 - Aug 4, 1926 Life is a school of good deeds where your ability to enter Nirvana is based upon your own good works.

64 - Aug 7, 1926 The evils of this earth are in fact the tactics of demons trying to corrupt your Holy progress. When the Dao opens evil forces are also released.

65 - Aug 9, 1926 Divine Orders command the first disciples to go to Can Giuoc to avert the evil that are corrupting the disciples there. . . .

67 - Aug 21, 1926 Divine teaching for disciples of Minh-Duong regarding the fact that one cannot attain enlightenment due to the closure of the Tao.

69 - Aug 22, 1926 Divine teaching to Mr Đ, who should repent and guide humanity.

70 - Aug 27, 1926 Each dignitary has to create their own divine family, and is responsible for the introduction of at least 12 people to the faith.

72 - Sept 11, 1926 You must be humble in order to save the beings of the world.

73 - Sept 17, 1926 Divine teaching regarding the building of the Divine Temple, of the thrones of the Giao Tong, Dau Su, Chuong Phap and of the universal globe.

74 - Sept 18, 1926 In Vietnam from now on there will be a true faith, the faith that God has established as the national religion.

75 - Sept 22, 1926 How to conquer evil.

76 - Sept 29, 1926 How to cultivate self to develop your personality and attitude.

78 - Oct 1, 1926 Divine teaching in French for a French guest.

80 - Oct 4, 1926 Divine teaching regarding the creation of one position of Buddha, three positions of Immortals, 36 positions of Saints, 72 positions of sages, and three thousand positions of disciples.

81 - Oct 12, 1926 Divine teaching regarding the wearing of plain clothes.

82 - Oct 24, 1926 God is Buddha, and Buddha is God. The three offerings: wine (khi), flowers (tinh) and tea (than).

84 - Sept 15, year of Yang Fire Tiger Ho Quang Chau's responsibility for spreading the Tao in central Viet nam, stressing that politics and the Tao can never work together.

85 - Oct 27, 1926 Divine teaching in French for French believers.

87 - Oct 28, 1926 Divine teaching in French for French believers.

89 - Oct 29, 1926 Divine teaching regarding the challenges set by the three lords with Ly Bach (Great Immortal Li Po) administering justice. Ly Bach then explains the power of justice.

92 - Nov 1, 1926 Divine teaching at the Minh Tan Cenacle by Thai Thuong Lao Quan, Te Thien Dai Thanh and Le Son the Holy Mother.

95 – Nov. 12, 1926 Miracle of reincarnation

96 - Nov 20, 1926 Ranks of the dignitaries and the method of election.

99 - Nov 23, 1926 Divine teaching explaining what happened at Tu Lam Pagoda.

100 - Nov 24, 1926 Further divine teaching explaining what happened at the Tu Lam Pagoda.

102 - Nov 28, 1926 Divine teaching in French for French guest.

104 - Dec 2, 1926 Divine teaching by Spiritual Giao Tong Ly Bach regarding the issue of males and females at the temple.

105 - Dec 6, 1926 One must take the Tao to the heart rather than being led by confusion as one tries to walk the spiritual path, waking too late to realize your own folly.

106 - Dec 6, 1926 The disincarnation of the dignitary Thuong Tuong Thanh.

107 - Dec 13, 1926 If you realize the preciousness of the Tao, you would cherish it.

108 - Dec 15, 1926 Divine teaching in French for French guest.

110 - Dec 17, 1926 Divine teaching in French for French guest.

112 - Dec 19, 1926 Divine teaching regarding the reincarnation cycle of humans and demons. If one does not practice the Dao, one cannot escape reincarnation.

116 - Dec 19, 26 Divine teaching in French regarding the true nature of nobility, richness and glory.

117 - Dec 20, 26 Establishment of the New Codes.

118 - Dec 24, 26 The reasons of the establishment of the New Codes.

119 - Dec 27, 26 Performing good deeds is in accord with the divine will, committing misdeeds is against the celestial laws. Right and wrong actions are recorded by the angels and saints for the final judgment.

120 - Jan 8, 27 Divine teaching encouraging adepts to use all their talents.

121 - Jan 10, 27 In order to accomplish one's mission, one must be patient and even abide suffering.

123 - Jan 16, 27 How to present and receive the New Canonical Law to and from the Spiritual Giao Tong.

125 - Jan 17, 27 God has founded the Tao in Vietnam for humans to reach their original positions.

126 - Jan 18, 27 One must abstain from alcohol.

128 - Jan 18, 27 Whoever recognizes the Tao is blessed, whoever does not is unfortunate.

128 - Jan 18, 27 Sermon from Than Hoang Bon Canh for the people of the My Loc village.

130 - Jan 22, 27 God granted a poem to male and female disciples.

132 - Jan 26, 27 One must cultivate self in order to escape reincarnation.

134 - Jan 31, 27 One must strive harder in order to reach the end of the Path.

135 - Feb 1, 27 You must concentrate in promoting the Way,

136 - Feb 1, 27 Divine teaching from the late Confucian Censor-Cardinal Tuong regarding his joy and happiness for the faith.

138 - Feb 1, 27 Congratulations and rewards from God to many disciples, the Spiritual Giao Tong grants ceremonial costumes to the College of women.

139 - Feb 5, 27 Spiritual Giao Tong Ly Bach prayed in vain for the amnesty of Saigon, Hue and Hanoi.

140 - Dec 24, 27 Divine teaching regarding self cultivation and mutual love.

142 - Feb 1927 Bodhisattva Kwan Yin suggests cooperation to guide the younger generation toward the Tao.
143 - Feb 1927 Ordination of the local genie as the Van Xuong position to govern the Hiep Ninh village.
144 - Feb 13, 27 The spiritual and temporal powers of the Hiep Thien Dai.
146 - Feb 19, 27 God would be pleased if disciples tried to build their merits.
147 - March 1, 27 The destination of the noble part of the human mind after the death of the physical body.
148 - March 5, 27 In order to be enlightened you must first gain enough merit by spreading the way and guiding human beings.
150 - April 5, 27 One has to have sincerity granted by God to guide humanity.
151 - April 12, 27 Whoever intends to disturb the Tao will be punished.
152 - April 15, 27 If you yourself choose not to walk then God will not carry you through your life.
153 - April 20, 27 Divine teaching from the spiritual Giao Tong Ly Bach that the hatred and indifference amongst followers of the Tao would create animosity between people leading to chaos.
154 – 27-4 Year Dinh Mao In upholding justice and applying the law, humanity would be exiled to hell for ever.
156 - May 29, 27 Divine teaching of the Spiritual Giao Tong Ly Bach explaining that the Tao is erected through the virtuous minds and humble behavior of the disciples, if humans are still running after materials, all the earned credits would be washed away.
157 - June 1, 27 Difficulties encountered in bringing the way to the next generation. Divine teaching regarding the stopping of séances.
158- July 1927 God has assembled immortals and Buddhas to establish the Tao in the South with a proscription of argument.

CONTENTS BOOK 2

159 - Year BD, 1926: What is the Tao?
160 - Year BD, 1926: Lý Thái Bạch teaches about Sub dignitary election.
161 - 12-6-Bính Dần. July 21 1926: The Supreme Being teaches: If all the world practiced their faiths, the world could change the divine will.
162 - 27-6-Bính Dần (Aug 4, 1926): The Supreme Being teaches: Visible matters may be destroyed, but the Nothingness couldn't be.
163 - No date: The 8th lady Immortal: The duty of virtuous person is to be selfless, to take care of the comfort of humanity.
165 - 6-8-Bính Dần (Sept 12, 1926): The Supreme Being teaches: When you are successful, don't be hasty to express joy, when you fail, don't be hasty in your sorrow.
166 - Sept 30, 1926 (Bính Dần): The Supreme Being teaches: Pay respect to Superior Spirits. Practice sincerity and justice.
167 - 15-8-Bính Dần (Sept 21, 1926): The Supreme Being teaches: if the Tao was established late, there would be damage for humanity.
168 - 9-9-Bính Dần (Oct 15, 1926): The Supreme Being teaches: Do not offend the Superior Spirits.
169 - Nov 11, 1926 Bính Dần: The Supreme Being teaches: You have to endure more sufferings in order to reach divine position.
170 - 14-10-Bính Dần Nov 18, 1926: The Supreme Being opens the female college.
171 - Dec 8, 1926 The Supreme Being teaches: we must love and help each other.
172 - Dec 11, 1926: The Supreme Being teaches self-cultivation and performance of human duty in order to reach Nirvana.
173 - Dec 12, 1926: The Supreme Being teaches that repentance is invaluable.

175 - Dec 14, 1926   The Supreme Being teaches: Services to humanity need to be accomplished to attain noble divine positions.

177 - Jan 3, 1927 The Supreme Being laments: Few persons bother to look for the holy way but many rush toward the evil way.

178 - Jan 8, 1927 The Supreme Being teaches: If I do not found the Third Universal Salvation to save the predestined souls, the whole world would be destroyed.

179 - Jan 21, 1927   The Supreme Being teaches: The Tao was founded to guide people back from the suffering world, but if they do not hurry to heed the Tao, they will be exiled into hell.

180 - Jan 22, 1927   The Supreme Being teaches: You must endeavor to fulfill your special responsibility in order to attain a noble position.

182 - 20-12-Bính Dần (Jan 23, 1927): The Supreme Being teaches: In following the path of the Tao, you will find a peaceful and contented life.

183 - 20-12-Bính Dần (Jan 23, 1927): The Supreme Being teaches: With perseverance, you cultivate self in the Holy way, you will reach the noble position.

20-12-Bính Dần (Jan 23, 1927): The Supreme Being teaches: Be patient, maintain your virtue, be good moral examples for future generations, earn merit by serving humanity so that at the end of your life, you will be able to return to your spiritual origins.

184 - 20-12-Bính Dần (Jan 23, 1927): The Supreme Being teaches: Try to cultivate yourself following religious rules in order to reach Nirvana.

186 - 12-1- Đinh Mão (Feb 13, 1927): The Supreme Being teaches: I founded the Great Way in the southern part of this country to compensate a country which has been greatly affected by My rage.

187 - 18-1-Đinh Mão (Feb 19, 1927): Teachings given by Quan Thánh Đế Quân, Quan Âm, and Lý Thái Bạch.

188 - 18-1-Đinh Mão (Feb 19, 1927): The Supreme Being teaches: You have to put all your heart into spreading the Tao and to love and to help each other.

189 - 19-1-Đinh Mão (Feb 20, 1927): The Supreme Being teaches: Misery and disasters from East to West, according to divine arrangement, will befall cruel countries that have generated animosities in this world.

190 - 20-1-Đinh Mão (Feb 21, 1927): The Supreme Being teaches: You have to work cooperatively with one another to walk the road to Eternity.

191 - 27-1-Đinh Mão (Feb 28, 1927): Lý Thái Bạch teaches about the construction plan for the Holy See.

193 - 2-3-1927 Đinh Mão: Lý Thái Bạch teaches: In order to surmount difficulties, you must have perseverance and dedication and try to put the Tao above all.

194 - 3-3-1927 Đinh Mão: The Supreme Being teaches: Use your merit to surmount obstacles and to reach Eternity.

195 - 3-3-1927 Đinh Mão: The Supreme Being teaches: You should work harder in order to surmount difficulties.

197 - 5-3-1927 Đinh Mão: Quan Âm teaches female disciples: You have to cooperate with each other in order to guide future generations.

198 - 5-3-1927 Đinh Mão: The Supreme Being teaches: You have to love and help each other while guiding humanity. If because of secular ambition, you become divided, hating and fighting each other, you would make poor examples to future generations.

200 - 4-2-Đinh Mão (Mar 7, 1927): The Supreme Being teaches: If the Tao were not created, people, because of their cruelty, would reincarnate again and again to pay their karma, and no one would be fully blessed.

202 - June 1, 1927: The Supreme Being teaches: At the end of this 6th month, I will stop all initiation séances, and from then on you have to use only your sincerity in order to spread the Tao.

203 - Sept 12, 1927 Đinh Mão: Lý Thái Bạch teaches: You should follow the holy teachings of the Great Mercy. You may submit to me the petition of promotion for whoever has closely followed the rules and regulations of the Sacerdotal Council.

205 - Sept 17, 1927 Đinh Mão: The Supreme Being teaches: I use peace and tranquility to lead you on the divine road, but if dignitaries are concerned more about titles and positions than cultivation of virtues, their punishment would be doubled.

207 - Oct 1, Đinh Mão (1927): The Supreme Being teaches: I have trained each of you so that you will have all authority to realize the divine will to lead humanity and to spread the Tao to all the world. Whether you fail or succeed, I would wait until the end to judge on your accomplished work.

209 - Oct 27, 1927 Đinh Mão: The Supreme Being teaches: In antiquity, many martyrs were not as well blessed and recognized as you are now. I just aspire you to love one another following My holy example. Love is the key to the thirty-six heavens, to Nirvana, and the White Jade Palace.

210 - Nov 29, 1927 Đinh Mão: The Supreme Being teaches: Before I stopped the séances, I had clearly given orders, but you did not deliver My words, and they became confused, it is your responsibility.

212 - End of the year Đinh Mão (1927): The Supreme Being teaches: I have worked hard to guide you in the Tao, and you keep giving Me disappointment every day. I wonder when you would succeed.

214 - Mậu Thìn 1928: Nhàn Âm Đạo Trưởng teaches: If you want to cultivate your virtues, you should start right at your heart.

215 - Feb 3, 1928 Mậu Thìn: The Supreme Being teaches: Anything consented to by all disciples pleases the divine will. I forbid you to set up séances or automatic writings.

217 - Mar 19, 1928 Mậu Thìn: Lý Thái Bạch teaches: If the title is granted to someone, this person would bear the title only, but there will never be two persons of the same title.

218 - 10-3-Mậu Thìn 1928: The Supreme Being teaches: Life is like an examination. If the examination is difficult, and yet you pass the examination with honors, your success would be more valuable.

219 - April 2, 1928 Mậu Thìn: The Supreme Being teaches: Each of you has an important responsibility to spread the Tao which, if you fail to fulfill, would lead to divine punishment according to the balance between your good and bad deeds.

220 - April 15, 1928 Mậu Thìn: The Supreme Being teaches: You should try your best to guide living being and fulfill your responsibility.

222 - April 16, 1928 Mậu Thìn: The Supreme Being teaches: I have treated all disciples as equals regardless of their titles

223 - April 23, 1928 Mậu Thìn: Teachings given by Thanh Tâm explaining the verses: No people walk the street or plough the field. No one is aware of the Tao; I fear for their destruction!

224 - 5-5-Mậu Thìn (June 22, 1928): The Supreme Being teaches: I am grieved by the division among you.

225 - 11-5-Mậu Thìn June 28, 1928: The Supreme Being teaches how to refine sugar in comparing sufferings to black sugar.

226 - 4-6-Mậu Thìn 1928: Tiêu Sơn Taoist teaches: Be cautious of your steps so that your efforts are not wasted.

228 - July 18, 1928 Mậu Thìn: Chơn Cực Lão Sư teaches about the destiny of the Tao.

230 - July 28, 1928 Mậu Thìn: The Supreme Being teaches: You would be awakened, realize you have strayed, and return to the right path.

232 - 19-6-Mậu Thìn (Aug 5, 1928): The Supreme Being teaches about the current situation of the Tao as a disease. Everyone likes to enjoy personal sovereignty and to fight against you.

234 - Year Mậu Thìn (1928): The Supreme Being teaches about precept "Not to kill"

235 - Year Mậu Thìn (1928): The Supreme Being teaches about precept "Not to steal"
237 - Year Mậu Thìn (1928): The Supreme Being teaches about precept "Not to be obscene".
238 - Jan 18, 1929 Mậu Thìn: The Supreme Being teaches about precept "Not to be drunk"
240 - Jan 18, 1929 Mậu Thìn: The Supreme Being teaches about precept "Not to sin by words"
241 - Year Kỷ Tỵ (Feb 10, 1929): The Supreme Being teaches: Your self-cultivation of virtue is stalled so that the congregation would be shattered.
242 - 7-3- Kỷ Tỵ (April 16, 1929): The Supreme Being teaches about the death of the Thượng Phẩm.
243 - Jan 11, 1930 (12-12- Kỷ Tỵ): The Supreme Being teaches: If you cannot love each other, I forbid you to hate each other.
244 - Feb 7, 1930 Canh Ngọ: The Supreme Being teaches: The practice of the Tao is the opposite of living the secular life in order to get closer to the divine illumination. You cannot practice the Tao and run after secular desires at the same time.
247 - April 12, 1930 Canh Ngọ: Nhàn Âm Đạo Trưởng explains the verses The rooster in the cage, although being fully fed every day, would not know when it is going to be slaughtered, While the crane, although not having enough to eat, is able to fly freely in the sky.
249 - April 21, 1930 (23-3-Canh Ngọ): The Supreme Being teaches: Try to cultivate your virtues in order to prevail against evils.
251 - June 8, 1930 Canh Ngọ: Quan Thánh Đế Quân teaches to return to the right path
253 - June 8, 1930 Canh Ngọ: Nhàn Âm Đạo Trưởng teaches to be awakened and spiritually strong to avoid destruction.
254 - June 10, 1930 (5-5-Canh Ngọ): Lý Bạch teaches that The Tao is not a commodity that you have to sell.
255 - Dec 24, 1930 Canh Ngọ: Lý Giáo Tông teaches: Because you bear a physical body, and therefore could not

withstand the full measure of oppression. But for myself, no power of this visible world could touch me. I have to use my divine eyes to recognize the situations for you.

257 - April 26, 1931 (9-2-Tân Mùi): The Supreme Being teaches: Understanding the divine will, understanding yourself, and understanding living beings are the ways to find the bright torch of the noble Tao's lighthouse, guiding you out of the ocean storm.

259 - Aug 1, 1931 Tân Mùi: Lý Giáo Tông teaches that he takes the responsibility of the Giáo Tông to set out the stepping stones for all his younger brothers and sisters to reclaim their positions.

261 - Dec 23, 1931 Tân Mùi: The Supreme Being teaches the Sacerdotal Council to fulfill the duty assigned by Thái Bạch. Any order from Thái Bạch and the Hộ Pháp should be studied thoroughly and implemented by the Sacerdotal Council and High Council.

263 - Mar 20, 1932 (14-2-Nhâm Thân): Nguyệt Tâm Chơn Nhơn teaches: Few souls appear at the gates of Heaven, but a myriad can be seen at the gates of Hell.

264 - Oct 1932 Nhâm Thân: The 8th lady Immortal teaches about the Yin energy.

265 - Feb 12, 1933: The 8th lady Immortal notifies about the final arrangements by the Supreme Being to preserve the destiny of living beings. The 6th lady Immortal teaches that all Superior Spirits are happy about the changes of the procedures.

266 – The 6th Female fairy of the Jasper Pond Palace

267 - 17-3-Quí Dậu 1933: Quan Âm teaches: The most precious element of the Tao is harmony.

268 - April 21, 1933 Quí Dậu: Quan Âm teaches: According to the love of life of the Great Merciful Father, we have to open the heart to love all living beings because they are all created by the Merciful Father.

269 - May 8, 1933 Quí Dậu: Quan Âm teaches: You should participate in worship ceremonies frequently in order to be attuned to Superior Spirits, to pray to the Great Mercy to forgive you and all living beings, to be receptive to the Great Mercy, and to open the loving kindness.

270 - May 26, 1933 Quí Dậu: Nguyệt Tâm Chơn Nhơn teaches: the Law is established. If you follow the laws, the organization would succeed; if not, it would fall into ruin.

271 - 9-4-Giáp Tý 1934: The 7th lady Immortal teaches about the Yin energy.

273 - July 20, 1934 Giáp Tý: The Supreme Being teaches about spiritism (conscious and unconscious mediums).

274 - 15-7-Giáp Tý 1934: The Cao Thượng Phẩm teaches: Please help people out from suffering. Don't make anyone suffer.

275 - 16-7-Giáp Tý 1934: Thái Thượng Đạo Tổ teaches about some indispensable secret matters.

278 - Nov 13, 1935 (18-10 Ất Hợi): Lý Thái Bạch congratulates the Hộ Pháp for his patience and hardship in improving the congregation.

280- INDEX

291- Contact information

COLLECTION OF SELECTED CAODAI HOLY MESSAGES

Foreword

In this last era, people have been caught up in the advances of a materialistic age which enhances their cravings for luxury goods, expensive foods, designer clothing, and the finest homes and vehicles they can attain. Such secular attractions spur vicious competition between human beings and among societies, with little thought of the future of the world or eternity for themselves; the only thing that seems to matter in life is that the strong prevail as the meek succumb to their interests. The powerful rich mercilessly oppress the poor and vulnerable in an age-old legacy of indulgence against all that is holy. Alas, history's wave of civilization has not promoted the good, rather shattering moral traditions and belief; life is used only to advance the profane-- death having no meaning except a lost opportunity to build wealth, giving no thought to a hereafter of Nirvana or Hades. The educated elite develop killing arms and lifesaving drugs that are only available to the rich; charity and service to humanity are paid little heed. Even loyalty to spouse and family have decayed through the excesses of materialism.

And so, out of Heaven was the Tao founded as an offer of redemption for human beings, reiterating eternal sanctity and morality for the modern age. Because of love for all Creation, The Supreme Being reveals the Tao through miraculous spiritism, using simple Vietnamese language. The disciples who were initiated since the time when spiritism ceased, could not have the pleasure of hearing these precious messages emanating from the Merciful Supreme Being.

Thus the Sacerdotal Council has selected and published these holy teachings for everyone. Its belief is that whoever receives these holy teachings would be filled with grace. Its hope is that all may cherish these invaluable words from Superior Spirits, putting their hearts into the reading of them in order to understand the miraculous Tao and to commit to self-cultivation and selfless love of the human family.

May whoever receives these holy words experience the divine light illuminating the path of their life.

Tayninh Holy See, the 21st day of the 10th month of the year Đinh Mão.
Respectfully.
The Sacerdotal Council

INTRODUCTION
to the translation of Thanh Ngon Hiep Tuyen

I am honored to have been asked to introduce readers to this translation of the spirit messages that make up the sacred scriptures of Caodaism, a new religion which is officially called the Great Way of the Third Age of Universal Redemption. After having studied Caodaism for over a decade, I can testify to the fact that is a fascinating new religion, born in colonial Indochina in 1926, which is now gathering increasing attention all over the world. These teachings were conveyed in an unusual way: Rather than being transmitted to any single individual, they were presented through a sort of dictation at spirit medium séances, through the use of a device called the phoenix basket (known in French as the corbeille a bec) and the efforts of two mediums. The movements of the phoenix basket trace out words and sentences, and this form of "spirit writing" is then interpreted and transcribed, so that it can serve to instruct others. The messages come from a range of divine beings, from the Jade Emperor (also known as Cao Dai, "the highest power") to the Invisible Pope (Ly Thai Bach, a famous Taoist poet from the Tang dynasty), to various other spirits, including the Sacred Mother of Humanity (Dieu Tri Kim Mau, also known as the Taoist Queen of the Heavens)

The corpus of spirit messages included in this collection are the officially selected messages which have been central to the formation of Caodaism. They are presented in verse, as well as prose, and the elaborate Sino-Vietnamese language used in them is sometimes challenging for even native speakers to understand. For this reason, it is especially valuable to have these translations, prepared so that a new generation can read the teachings and understand them even if they are not fluent in Vietnamese. The translators have worked for many decades to develop and refine these translations, and their efforts will allow scholars and members of the public to get a much better understanding of the content of Caodai scriptures.

There have now been a number of studies which have tried to explain the history, theology and rituals of Caodaism to a wider audience, but of course the most direct way to learn about Caodai beliefs is to read these teachings yourself.

Janet Alison Hoskins
Professor of Anthropology and Religion
University of Southern California

Foreword of the translators

The diversity of religions brings about an array of uncertainties and mistrust between people of different traditions. CaoDai propounds the goal to unite religions in harmony and peace and to solve human conflicts. It conceives that all humans are brothers and sisters from the same Father God. Each and every member of the human race has God's spirit inside, and with cultivation, this spirit will be reunited with its noble origin.

Via spiritism, CaoDai receives words from the Supreme Being under the form of poems and prose teaching humanity ways of life to reach peace within and without.

We translate these teachings into English in the hope that many may be blessed with wonderful miraculous words from the Merciful Supreme Being.

Hum D. Bui, MD
Hong D. Bui, MD

*The Eye represents the heart,
Source of twin light beam
Light and Spirit are One
God is the Spirit's gleam*

The noble effort of CaoDai is to unite all of humanity through a common vision of the Supreme Being, whatever our minor differences, in order to promote peace and understanding throughout the world. CaoDai does not seek to create a gray world, where all religions are exactly the same, only to create a more tolerant world, where all can see each other as sisters and brothers from a common divine source reaching out to a common divine destiny realizing peace within and without.

BOOK I
HOLY MESSAGES

Christmas, 1925:

JADE EMPEROR, or CAO DAI TIEN ONG DAI BO TAT MA HA TAT, TEACHING THE GREAT WAY FOR THE SOUTHERN QUARTER

I have reigned supreme for millennia.

Those who improve themselves spiritually will receive blessings.

The miraculous way has been taught and followed Throughout the world for millennia.

Rejoice this day, the 24th of December, the anniversary of my arrival in Europe to teach the Way! Your allegiance brings much joy to me. Blessings will fill this house. The time has come, so be ready to receive my instruction. More miracles will manifest to further persuade you.

Raise high the flag of guidance for all living beings--the born and the unborn!

The Way has been successfully shown;

Those who improve themselves spiritually will return to Heaven

In the palace of splendor.

CHIEU KY TRUNG *do dan* HOAI SANH

BAN *dao khai* SANG QUI GIANG *thanh*;

HAU DUC TAC CU *thien dia canh*.

HUON MINH MAN** *dao thu dai danh*.

** *The capital letter words are the names of the first 12 disciples of the Supreme Being. The last three names of the last verse are the names of the seance participants*

January 3 1926:

JADE EMPEROR, OR CAODAI TIEN ONG DAI BO TAT MA HA TAT, TEACHING THE GREAT WAY FOR THE SOUTHERN QUARTER:

SPIRITISM OR AUTOMATIC WRITING.

In spiritism, the medium must meditate deeply so that his spirit will then be able to come to Me, listen to My instructions, and have his body to write down the messages.

What is a spirit?

The spirit is your second body. It is very difficult for the spirit of a human being to transcend the physical body. The spirits of Saints, Immortals, and Buddhas are very marvelous and immortal. The spirit of an enlightened person may transcend the body and even travel the universe. Only the spirit may approach Me. When the basket with beak is used in spiritism, if the person is unconscious, the spirit may then leave the physical body, hear My instructions, and have the body transcribe the messages. If the interpreter's reading is incorrect, the medium's spirit will not agree with the interpretation. They will be obliged to write again. In the other form of spiritual contact known as automatic writing, or inspired writing, I will come to you and make your spirit unstable for a while. During that time, your spirit will be able to listen to Me. Your hand will obey and write. In this form of spiritual contact, I cooperate with you so that you can reach Universal Truths.

Before the session, one must purify both mind and body-do not omit this purification or you risk failure. To practice well, one should keep one's mind pure, not encumbered by everyday living matters, and keep the hands cleansed and deodorized. Deep meditation will allow one's spirit to transcend the body and communicate with Me.

The mediums should be chosen for their advanced spirit so that the session will be fruitful. They should practice vegetarianism, and train themselves toward being completely balanced (as good as Saints, Immortals, and Buddhas) to be able to properly achieve the purpose of the session and transmit the teachings. They are considered My assistants in the propagation of the Way. Spiritual contact cannot be taken lightly. In the reception of vibrations from the spirit, each person has personal vibrations which may be influenced by their own emotions and personality and may interfere: subsequently these writings may not be correct. One should take caution in setting up sessions and in recognizing the authenticity of the writings.

So, after each spiritism session, you have to wait for My approval before any implementation.

February 20, 1926:

JADE EMPEROR, OR CAO DAI TIEN ONG DAI BO TAT MA HA TAT, TEACHING THE GREAT WAY TO THE SOUTHERN QUARTER:

From My precious throne, flowers are happily and continually blooming more.

Although many different branches are growing out, they will belong later to one same family.

Likewise, you should join together to try your best in serving the Great Way.

With patience and loyalty, you will come back to Me.

It is not easy to find the Way to Nirvana.

I have in My hands all miracles of the universe. In antiquity, to find Nirvana, one had to cultivate one's self over the course of innumerable lives.

Now, anyone from all over the world can be guided to this Way,

Whose virtuous messengers I am still discovering.

Attempting to change the hearts of the evil ones has brought me sorrow on many occasions.

If one wishes to escape from the suffering world, One should cultivate one's spiritual self and thus will find Nirvana soon.

The branches that you are now are all part of Me. You will understand this later. I am happy to see you always getting along well with each other: it is a precious gift to Me. Be united and be cooperative in glorifying the Way. My Way is you, and you are Me. Be united and strong. Do not quarrel. Keep performing your duties and you will more fully know My will later.

Being brothers, you should love each other.

The more virtuous you are, the higher spiritual accomplishments you may attain.

You have to be determined to continue on your way to Nirvana.

You all have the same flesh and blood.

You should understand how miraculous I am. To teach, you have to use skillful and varied means, depending upon the level of the intelligence of the people. The one who does not have enough intelligence will not understand if you present doctrines too advanced for him or her.

I forbid you to criticize others, especially your disciples. Remember that I Myself am in them.

You do not need to have the same name to be in the same family.

By following the same Way, you all have the same father. In this life span of one hundred years, remember to serve humanity,

And try your best to teach each other Concordance.

Wait for My orders. Your duty and responsibility were predetermined.

I start to teach you now...

In *Bach Ngoc Kinh* (White Pearl Palace), there are males and females. Female Buddhas and Immortals are even more powerful than their male counterparts.

Tr..., you have a mission, I will be with you and within you wherever you go. Whatever you are teaching people is considered as from ME. You have to be flexible. You alone are not enough to convince people. You have to help everybody of any sex, from any country to learn My Way. Do not be too strict with them at the beginning. Remember that every living being, including materials and plants, will all eventually be convinced when they listen to My Holy messages through you. Don't worry.

The sun rises from the horizon.
Get together and be ready to start.
Learn the Great Way from the Great Teacher.
You will return to Me at the end of this long, long road.

I have been telling you that I have prepared everything in your heart: Whatever you have in your mind was already predetermined. You need not worry. The Way is reserved for predetermined people.

Whoever has worshipped the Demonic Spirit cannot be My disciples.

If there is good, there has to be bad.
It is difficult to distinguish between the two.
Human beings therefore must come to Me
To become Immortals and Buddhas.

If you have already spent all your accumulated blessings and violated God's laws, you are in no way forgiven. If you could not even escape from the secular laws and justice on earth, how could you escape from God's laws? Being your Father, I have to be just and to punish you. Think about punishment and behave yourself. Remember that God is impartial: Don't rely on your Great and Gentle Father to become disrespectful to Him.

February 23, 1926

To teach children, teach yourself first

The work of education is as important as the work of giving birth.
In each person, there is a part of my spirit
That I cherish and that you have to educate.
That spiritual part then becomes part of society.

February 25, 1926
THE JADE EMPEROR, or CAO DAI TIEN ONG DAI BO TAT MA HA TAT, TEACHING THE GREAT WAY TO THE SOUTHERN QUARTER.

Disciple Trung, come into the middle of the room and prostrate before me.
Well done. However, you must remember to pray "NAM MO CAO DAI TIEN ONG DAI BO TAT MA HA TAT" each time you nod.
A major ceremony has three offerings: incense and flowers, wine, and tea.
You offer all of these yourself.
As you prostrate, put your hands together with your left thumb pointing at the Ty position [position of the Year of the Mouse] at the base of the ring finger, and with your left hand resting on the upturned right hand underneath.
Henceforth, you are required to wear a special blue costume with large sleeves, askew collar and nine belts. You must also wear cloth shoes. Others wear no shoes.
Why prostrate?
To show your respect.
Why place your hands together in such a manner?
The left hand represents Yang, the sun; the right hand represents Yin, the moon. The combination of Yin and Yang is the Dao, the principle for the creation and evolution of the universe.
Why prostrate twice before a living person?
Two represents the Yin and Yang combined, or the *Dao*.

Why prostrate four times before a dead person?

Two prostrations are for the person, one is for heaven and one is for the earth.

Why prostrate three times before Saints and Genies? Because they are the third rank of the celestial classes. This pattern also indicates the unification of *Tinh* (physical matter), *Khi* (emotions), and *Than* (spirit), which is the Dao itself.

Why prostrate nine times before Buddhas and Immortals? Because they are the creators of the nine heavens. Why, then, must you prostrate 12 times before Me? You could not understand. Because I am the Emperor of the universe and have twelve Zodiacs in My hands. Number 12 is thus My own number.

It is not time to understand the full meaning of the Divine Eye, but I will briefly explain this to you.

"The heart manifests at the eye

Presiding everything are two sources of light (Yin and Yang);

Light is spirit;

Spirit is God."

Since the *Dao* was established, there has been a lack of the spirit in the miraculous mechanism of enlightenment. With this third salvation, I will allow the *Than* (spirit) to be unified with the *Tinh* (physical matter) and the *Khi* (emotions), leading to a unification of the three elements, which is itself the miraculous mechanism of the enlightenment.

Remember to explain this to disciples.

The positions of Genies, Saints, Immortals, and Buddhas have been unchanged since the *Dao* was established: so has the technique of spiritual self-improvement, but the *Than* was not allowed to be unified with Tinh and Khi, so that there was no more enlightenment.

I come today to authorize this unification so that you may reach enlightenment.

You now understand that the *Than* (spirit) is located at the Eye. Explain this to the disciples. The Eye, or the *Than* (spirit), is the origin of Immortals and Buddhas.

Remember My name when you preach.

March 13, 1926

THE JADE EMPEROR, or CAO DAI
TEACHING THE GREAT WAY
TO THE SOUTHERN QUARTER.

I inform you now so that you will not be able to claim that I am unable to enforce My rules on my disciples.

Remember that there is falsehood as well as truth. There cannot be one without the other. (divine smile)

Remember that it is very hard to become a worthy disciple: The more I love, the more I challenge. In order to reach Nirvana, you must be worthy; otherwise, you will end in Hell. Love, love, hatred, hatred...Who knows?

Therefore, it is not because I hate that I will not teach, and it is not because I love that I will not seduce. Remember that I have sent many wild beasts to surround you and to bite you every day; but do not worry, because I have already given you an armor for your protection which they can never see and which is your virtue. Always keep it until you return to Me. Remember and obey.

Vinh Nguyen Tu, April 7, 1926

THE JADE EMPEROR, or CAO DAI TIEN ONG DAI BO TAT MA HA TAT, TEACHING THE GREAT WAY TO THE SOUTHERN QUARTER.

Nhien Dang Co Phat (Dipankara Buddha) is Me.

Sakya Muni is Me.

Thai Thuong Nguon Thi (previous life of Lao Tse) is Me.

Who is CaoDai?

April 8, 1926

Sakya Muni's spiritual messages:

Sakya Muni

Moves Buddhist principle,

Moves Buddhist laws,

Moves Buddhist disciples

To the original "GREAT WAY"

For all living beings.

Great joy! Great joy!

All Angels, Saints, Immortals, and Buddhas are very joyful for the opportunity to be in this third universal salvation! I will not worry any more about suffering in this world, because all living beings are receiving teachings from the Jade Emperor, or Cao Dai Tien Ong Dai Bo Tat Ma Ha Tat!

CAO DAI

Lich*, did you hear Sakya Muni? What is *"Tam Ky Pho Do?"*

It is the Third Universal Salvation.

Why is it called *"Pho Do?"*

"Pho" means to expose the Great Way, and *"Do"* means to save all living beings.

How is the Great Way exposed and how are living beings saved? What are living beings?

Living beings are not a selected group of people as you thought, but include all of humanity. In order to spread the Great Way and to save humanity, the precious principle must be exposed to all people.

Therefore, you must practice meditation well, so you can accompany Trung** this May to spread the Great Way. Listen and obey.

You will wear a costume similar to Trung's, but in red.

*Lich is the name of the "Dau Su" (Cardinal) of the Confucian Branch.
**Trung is the name of the "Dau Su" of the Taoist Branch.

April 22nd and 23rd, 1926
The 11th and 12th of the 3rd month of the year of Yang Fire Tiger

THE JADE EMPEROR, or CAO DAI TIEN ONG DAI BO TAT MA HA TAT, TEACHING THE GREAT WAY FOR THE SOUTHERN QUARTER.

You three, my children, listen about your next heavenly duties. Are you happy?

One day late in promoting the faith is one more harmful day for humanity. Although I am concerned, it is the will of your Creator that we will have difficulties spreading the faith. So, Trung, Cu, and Tac, you three should organize in the following way:

Listen Trung: you must move the tablet of Ly Bach to underneath my representation on the altar. Then place a chair next to the altar, and another chair on top of it for the throne of the *Giao Tong*. Place three other chairs on the lower level for the thrones of the three *Dau Su*. Cover these three chairs to keep them clean. Place the *Giao Tong*'s celestial costume on the top chair. Place the azure costume (for the Taoist *Dau Su*) on the middle chair, and the red costume (for the Confucian *Dau Su*) on the right chair. Write the word *"Thai"* (representing the Buddhist *Dau Su*) on paper and paste it on the back of the chair on left.

At my table, in front of the thrones of the three *Dau Su*, place a chair with a tablet inscribed with the following words: *"Cuu Thien Cam Ung Loi Thinh Pho Hoa Thien Ton"* (The Lord of Thunder and of Spreading of the teachings of the Nine Heavens) with a *Kim Quang Tien* charm hanging in the middle.

Place the séance table in front of the table of the Five Thunder Lords. After the séance, move the séance table away to create space for the two *Dau Su* to kneel to take their oaths.
Place another table by the front window. Listen, Cu: have Tac clean and deodorize himself and dress neatly with a hat . . . (celestial laughter).

Theoretically, he should wear armor, as in the theater, but it is so expensive that I have excused it. Tac must stand on the table facing the throne of the *Giao Tong*. His head should be covered with a 9 dm. red cloth. Make a *Giang Ma Xu* charm for him to hold. From now on you must purify yourself until the date of taking the oath. Cu, when you place the three celestial costumes on the appropriate thrones, you must hold incenses like you did previously for Me to summon the angels to guard these costumes and thrones. Then order the two *Dau Su* to kneel in front of their throne for Me to draw charms on their bodies. After praying, the two *Dau Su* must prostrate in front of Me 12 times and in front of the *Giao Tong* nine times. Then, Giang must announce "Take a seat," and then the *Dau Su* will sit down.

All disciples then kneel down in three groups. Tac must climb up to his table while you hold the incenses and come to the table of the Five Thunder Lords for Me to summon them. You then proceed to Tac so I can extract his spirit. Remember, Hau and Duc must deodorize their hands in order to be prepared to prevent Tac from falling. Order the two *Dau Su* to step down from their thrones, kneel in front of the table of the Five Thunder Lords, immediately in front of the *Kim Quang Tien* charm, put their hands (joined at the forehead) and take the following oath:

"I am Le Van Trung, whose religious name is Thuong Trung Nhut and Le Van Lich whose religious name is Ngoc Lich Nguyet, before heaven and earth and the Five Thunder

Lords, vow to fulfill the duty of guiding all our CaoDai brothers and sisters on the Divine Way, always strictly obeying the orders of our Master without straying onto the wrong path or establishing a deviant tradition. If we commit sins, we will be destroyed by the Five Thunder Lords."

Then kneel at the *Ho Phap* table and make the same vow, except the last sentence shall be:

"If we violate the Divine laws, we will be punished by the Ho Phap, our soul shall not be able to be liberated, and shall be reincarnated to the third lower spiritual level.

Then Giang will announce, "Take a seat," and the two *Dau Su* will return to their thrones. The disciples will prostrate two times in front of them.

Then each disciple will come to the front of the table of the Five Thunder Lords to take the following oath:

"I, (name)........, vow that from now on, I will follow the CaoDai faith unswervingly, united harmoniously with all disciples and following CaoDai laws. If I change my mind, I will be destroyed by the sky and the earth."

Then take the same oath in front of the *Ho Phap* table and then prostrate in front of the two *Dau Su*.

April, 24 1926

JADE EMPEROR or CAO DAI TIEN ONG DAI BO TAT MA HA TAT, TEACHING THE WAY FOR THE SOUTHERN QUARTER.

Formerly, people lacked transportation and therefore did not know each other, I then founded at different epochs and in different areas, five branches of the Great Way: the way of humanity, the way of Angels, the way of Saints, the way of Immortals, and the way of Buddhas, each based on the customs of the race. In present days, transportation has been improved, and people have come to know each other. But people do not always live in harmony because of the very multiplicity of those religions.

That is why I have decided to unite all those religions into one to bring them to the primordial unity. Moreover, the Holy Doctrine has been, through centuries, more and more denatured by the people responsible for spreading it. I am so broken-hearted to see that human beings, for the last ten thousand years, have sinned and subsequently suffered life after life in Hell.

I have now firmly resolved to come Myself to save you and not to leave anymore the Holy Doctrine in human hands. You have to be well organized to guide and support each other on your way to Nirvana.

I create then the *"Giao Tong"* position (Pope) who is the eldest brother of all dignitaries from the *"Giao Huu"* (Priest) to the *"Dau Su"* (Cardinal). No one in this world is allowed to have My authority to manage the human spirits. Whoever has well self cultivated will be worth the position I give. Otherwise, all disciples are all equal, and should not establish any sect or party; whoever commits crimes will be excluded from the religion.

April 26th, 1926
The 15th day of the 5th month of the year of the Yang Fire Tiger

JADE EMPEROR or CAO DAI TIEN ONG DAI BO TAT MA HA TAT, TEACHING THE WAY FOR THE SOUTHERN QUARTER.

Today you have not yet returned to your inner Divine Light.
Understanding people's hearts is hard;
You must wait until your enlightenment.
Because right now you are still not virtuous enough,
and others are wild.

Duc and Hau are appointed as *Tien Dao* Medium Assistant Taoists.
Cu is appointed as *Tien Hac* Medium Assistant Taoist.
Tac is appointed as Protector Fairy Medium Assistant Taoist.
Trung and Lich are already appointed: keep following My orders.
Ky is appointed as *Tien Sac Lang Quan, Giao Su* responsible for teaching.
Ban is appointed as *Tien Dao Cong Than,* Lecturer Taoist.
Cu, implement My orders!

Truong Sanh Temple (Can Giuoc) Sunday, May 30, 1926
The 19th Day of the 4th Month of the Year of the Yang Fire Tiger.

JADE EMPEROR or CAO DAI TIEN ONG DAI BO TAT MA HA TAT, TEACHING THE WAY FOR THE SOUTHERN QUARTER.

I could not believe that you, My disciples, could be so confused!
What is the meaning of *"Chieu Ky Trung do dan Hoai Sanh"* (Raise high the flag of guidance for all living beings --the born and the unborn)? It means that you have to help all living beings, including even the unborn.
Why did you chase disciples away?
Promise to admit! Open the door!
Listen, all living beings:
Formerly, I incarnated and created Buddhism almost six thousand years ago, and the Buddhist teachings have now been almost denatured. People even used to say that the Buddha did not teach. Today, I have decided not to incarnate anymore, but instead to use miracles to perfect Buddhism and to teach people. Thus, those living beings who do not wish to spiritually improve themselves and who will subsequently be punished in Hell will not deny their crimes and will not have any basis to blame Me by claiming that Buddha did not teach.
You must know that if you do not take the opportunity of this third universal salvation to improve yourself spiritually, you will have no more hope to be saved.
I will now reorganize the manner of worship:
You will set up an altar for Me in the middle of the temple between the altars of Quan Am Bo Tat and Quan Thanh De Quan. Thus, the statue of Quan Am Bo Tat (Bodhisattva Kuan Yin/Guan Yin Ru Lai) will be on my right, and the statue of Quan Thanh De Quan (Kuan Kung/Guan Gong/Guan Sheng Di Jun) will be on my left. On the next

row beneath will be different statues of other Buddhas, Immortals, and Saints. The t
uuemple will now be named, "Jade Emperor Temple."

Monday, May 31, 1926
20th day of the 4th month of the year of the Yang Fire Tiger

JADE EMPEROR or CAO DAI TIEN ONG DAI BO TAT MA HA TAT, TEACHING THE WAY FOR THE SOUTHERN QUARTER.

Trung, you must now go to G's house to organize the new way of worshipping until we establish new laws.

G., congratulations to you.

The spirit of the Divine is constant, regardless of the circumstances. That is what distinguishes you from the other, ordinary people. Ordinary people think of their birth country as their point of origin, even if they have not been there since they were children. However, the Saints think of Nirvana as their point of origin, even after they have incarnated into this world; otherwise, why would they deign to descend into this world to save ordinary human beings? You, too, could return to Nirvana if you cultivate yourself spiritually. To accomplish this, you should think about the millions of human beings who could not escape from the reincarnation cycle and have compassion toward them in order to save them.

Hoi Phuoc Tu (Can Giuoc),
the fifth of the 4th month of the year of the Yang Fire Tiger.
Saturday, the fifth of June 1926

JADE EMPEROR OR CAO DAI TIEN ONG DAI BO TAT MA HA TAT, TEACHING THE GREAT WAY FOR THE SOUTHERN QUARTER

Cu, read the spiritual messages,
Tac, recite the Karma prayers,
Sakya Muni is Me, I come to save living beings under the name Cao Dai Tien Ong Dai Bo Tat Ma Ha Tat.
Are you aware of this?
My disciple, The Dau Su (Cardinal) of the Buddhist branch, did not know the principles of spiritual self-cultivation in meditation. I sent the Dau Su of the Confucian branch to teach him.
Those thirty four disciples don't know the truth of meditation either. I will supervise their education. Obey.
You should all take these lessons.

SAKYA MUNI OR CAO DAI TIEN ONG DAI BO TAT MA HA TAT.

Listen, disciples
Since Luc To (the 6th Buddhist Master), the teaching of Buddhism was unavailable. Therefore, no one could reach Nirvana in spite of hard self-cultivation. Than Tu modified and denatured the original doctrine.
The original doctrine was lost for three thousand years and because of Karmic law, I have left it alone. This is now the time for the third universal salvation; *Ngoc Hu* Palace has ordered the saving of living beings. This was predicted clearly in the Buddhist Canon. You were not aware of it simply because you did not make the effort to discover it.
Alas! Lots of people suffered by failed attempts at spiritual self-cultivation. It hurts Me!

I am coming not only to save all living beings but also save other higher spirits such as Genies, Saints, Immortals, Buddhas who had to reincarnate to this world to complete their missions.

All living beings who have an opportunity to be with this third universal salvation should try their best to cultivate their spiritual selves. Success depends on yourselves. The original Buddhist way of cultivation seemed completely wrong at the time. Living beings became confused and disoriented, following the false doctrine of Than Tu for self-cultivation without success. I am coming to reveal to you this miraculous way. You need only follow it to attain enlightenment. Henceforth, you will not be able to blame anyone that you have not received My teachings.

Mardi, 8 Juin 1926
26 tháng tư Bính Dần

Ngọc-Hoàng Thượng-Đế Viết Cao-Đài
Giáo Đạo Nam Phương

CAO-ĐÀI

(Hai người Langsa hầu đàn)
Ce n'est pas ainsi qu'on se présente devant Dieu.

THĂNG

Tái cầu.

Cao-Đài, Le Très Haut

Ô! Race bénite! Je vais satisfaire ta curiosité. Humains, savez-vous d'où vous veniez?

Parmi toutes les créatures existant sur ce globe terrestre, vous êtes les plus bénis; je vous élève jusqu'à Moi en esprit et en sagesse. Vous avez toutes preuves pour vous reconnaître par promotion céleste.

Le Christ est venu parmi vous. Il versait son saint sang pour la rédemption. Quel profit avez-vous pendant presque deux mille ans de son absence? Vous préchez son Évangile sans même le comprendre. Vous dénaturez la signification de sa sainte doctorine. L'humanité souffre des vicissitudes de tous ses apôtres. Ils n'ont pas su suivre le même chemin du calvaire de leur Maître.

Le trône le plus précieux du monde est celui du premier de ses disciples. Cette doctorine, au lieu d'apporter à l'humanité la paix et la concorde, lui apporte la dissension et la guerre. Voilà pourquoi je viens vous apporter moi-même la paix tant promise.

Le Christ ne revient qu'ensuite.

Au revoir.... Vous apprendrez encore beaucoup de choses après de mes disciples.

Tuesday, June 8, 1926
the 26th day of the 4th month of the year of the Yang Fire Tiger

JADE EMPEROR OR CAO DAI TIEN ONG DAI BO TAT MA HA TAT,
TEACHING THE GREAT WAY TO THE SOUTHERN QUARTER CAODAI

(Present at the séance, there were also two French citizens). This is not the way that one presents oneself in front of God.
Ascension.
Re-evocation.

CaoDai, the Supreme.

O Blessed Race, I would satisfy your curiosity. Humans, do you know from whence you came?

Among all the creatures on the earth today, you are the most blessed; I have raised you almost to Me in spirit and in wisdom. You have all the proof you need to recognize your station in the cosmos.

Christ came among you. He shed his holy blood for your Salvation. Why have you drawn away from him during the almost two thousand years of his absence? You preach his Good News without understanding it. You have weakened the meaning of his holy teachings. Humanity suffers from the whims of all these false teachers. If only they had followed the same path of Calvary as their Master!

The most precious throne in all the world is that of the first of the true disciples. This teaching, instead of bringing peace and harmony to humanity, has brought it dissension and war.

And so this is why I myself have come to bring you the peace you were promised.

Christ can only return then.

You will understand more things from my disciples.

Good bye.

June 27th, 1926
The 18th day of the 5th month of the year of the Yang Fire Tiger

JADE EMPEROR, or CAO DAI TIEN ONG DAI BO TAT MA HA TAT, TEACHING THE GREAT WAY FOR THE SOUTHERN QUARTER.

Nhon, now you are to start practicing music until the day of the séance at Vinh Nguyen Tu. For the ceremony opening, do not use the *Bat Nha* drums (small drums) but the *Ngoc Hoang Sam* drum (Jade Emperor Thunder drum) in twelve rounds with twelve strikes for each round.

The *Bach Ngoc Chung* (White Pearl Bell) is to be struck the same way.

At the ceremony convening, when "Start Music" is announced, you will play all seven pieces of music and drums. At the offerings, play three *Nam Xuan* pieces (South Spring); and the student priests (who are bringing the offerings) will walk seven steps following the character *Tâm* (Heart). For the chanting you will play the *"Dao Ngu Cung"* pieces. Lich, I have given all instruction about rituals in the "New Codes." You must teach that to all disciples for them to follow during ceremony. Nghia, you must learn the announcements by heart. Tell Duc to do the same. You three children have to remember well My instruction. Those children--Nghia, Hau, Duc, Trang, Cu, Tac, and Sang--have to wear white clothing and stand in this order: Nghia and Duc, as announcers, will stand the outermost at the Ho Phap altar. Then Hau and Trang will form the next circle. Then the next three: Tac in the middle, Cu on right and Sang on left. Lich will arrange the celebrants for the three inside altars as follows:

The Taoist in the middle,
The Confucian on the right,
The Buddhist on the left.

The tablets of deceased disciples are to be arranged next to My altar according to their branches. Ky and Kim, as the inner announcers, will stand at the inside altar: Ky on the right, Kim on the left. Ban and Gioi are the first pair of student priests and will walk in the middle with another pair, who are Ty and Tiep. Next will be Nhon and Trung on the left, Giang and Kinh on the right.

There should be three tables outside for the three offerings. At the announcement from inside, the student priests will bring the offerings from the three tables from outside to the offering dignitaries inside. Trung, you will ask the two elders of the Minh Duong sect to stand inside as the Taoist receivers. The Confucian receivers will be Kinh and Chuong. I will choose the Buddhist receivers later on that day. (Laughter)

I will tell Minh to come. (Laughter)

At the three tables outside, there should be two offering dignitaries for each table. Tuong and Tuoi will be the Taoist offering dignitaries. Muoi and Van will be the Confucian offering dignitaries. I will choose the Buddhist offering dignitaries on that day. (Laughter)

Ban, stand up. Let Me draw the character *"Tâm"* (heart) first so I can show you how to signify the character with your feet.

(Use your right toes for the first stroke, then lift your right leg. Then move it horizontally as a comma. Stand so that your two feet are at the same horizontal line. Make the strokes now. Move backward a little)

Cu, show him your steps.

Children, watch Me step.

Hieu, bring Me some water.

Why did your step make a reverse character?

Cu, you step correctly. Repeat.

Very well, Cu, it should be so. In order to have a more elegant movement, when you stroke your toes, you bounce the body a little. (Laughter)

Very well, Ban. The Master continues. Read again, Nghia.

As the outer announcers say "Tea," then "Kneel," the dignitaries kneel down, put the tea offering at the level above the head. A pair of student priests holds candles and steps forward. When "Kneel" is announced next, they stroke the left foot, raise the right leg and kneel down at the same rhythm with the other three pairs of student priests; when the drum and music start again, they all stand up at the same time and face the altar.

...It has to be so, children...After standing up and facing the altar, the student priests hold the candles and the offerings at their chest. At the second round of drums, they raise the candles and the offerings up and start their seven steps (following the character *"Tâm"*) according to the drum rhythm. I will tell Nhon to drum for you at that time. (Laughter)

Trung, follow the New Codes for the ceremony.

July 5th, 1926

CAODAI

K..., Listen to Me, your Master.

People on earth, in order to be rich, you find ways to make money. This is solely from the material point of view. The Angels, Saints, Immortals, and Buddhas, in order to be enlightened, must gain service credits.

I come to save you by establishing a school of credits and of virtues for your spiritual development and enlightenment. Whether or not you become enlightened is totally up to you. Listen to Me! K...If you don't go through My school, you can never be enlightened anywhere else.

My child K...! Very few people go by the White Pearl Gate, but many go to Hell. Think about it and cultivate your spirit. As much as I love you now, so much more will you regret in the future not listening to me when you could.

I have already forgiven you because I know that you will have repented.

Your mission is great. Wait for My orders at the Ngoc Dan (name of a séance).

July 15, 1926

JADE EMPEROR, or CAO DAI TIEN ONG DAI BO TAT MA HA TAT, TEACHING THE GREAT WAY FOR THE SOUTHERN QUARTER.

Cu and Tac, you must bring four children, and find eight other local children. Place three of them on each side as follows:
        An.........East side.
        Bich......West side.
        Tri.........South side.
        Hoang...North side.
Have each of them hold a little flag, as follows: blue, red, white, yellow, black--three flags per each side. You three will hold the flags in the center. If there is not enough time to make flags in fabric, you may use colored paper, 9 dm. in length, 3 dm. in width. Cut them diagonally. Listen and obey.

After everything is arranged in order, Cu will hold the incenses for Me to summon the angels. After that, tell Van to stay inside until the end. If you step out your mind may become unstable.

Tell the children to meditate deeply. Obey! Tac: You must watch them closely at all times.

Have Lich distribute flags to the children, because it is his duty to read the mantra while doing so.

Saturday, July 17, 1926
The 8th of the sixth month of the year of the Yang Fire Tiger

JADE EMPEROR, or CAO DAI TIEN ONG DAI BO TAT MA HA TAT, TEACHING THE GREAT WAY FOR THE SOUTHERN QUARTER.

Lady Duong, I, your Master, assign you to establish the Female College. Your gender alone does not condemn you to the kitchen.

At this 3rd Universal Salvation, there will be much hard work for everyone. Male and female are of equal number. Not only males work to become Immortals and Buddhas. As I have said, at the *Bach Ngoc Kinh* (White Pearl Palace), there are both male and female, and frequently, females are predominant.

So follow My order to establish the Female College. Listen and obey! I will always be with you. Don't worry.

H., I assign you to teach and guide all the females. I will share some responsibility with you.

Ngoc Dan (Can Giuoc)
Saturday, July 17, 1926
The 8th day of the sixth month of the year of the Yang Fire Tiger

JADE EMPEROR, or CAO DAI TIEN ONG DAI BO TAT MA HA TAT, TEACHING THE GREAT WAY FOR THE SOUTHERN QUARTER.

My greetings to all disciples.
Great Joy! Great joy!
The *Dau Su* (Cardinal) of the Confucian Branch may teach secret principles. Whoever practices vegetarianism for more than ten days per month may receive these secret, precious teachings. All disciples should practice vegetarianism. Why? It is not simply that I wish to adhere to tradition and enforce an old law, but that this law is important, or you could never reach the stage of Immortal or Buddha without it. Allow Me to explain:
Everyone on this earth has two bodies. The earthly one is called the physical; the sacred body, the spiritual. The spiritual body is formed from the earthly body and therefore may be visible or invisible. This miraculous spiritual body is formed from *"Tinh," "Khi"* and *"Than"* by spiritual self-cultivation. This spiritual body is lighter than air. When it leaves the physical body, it retains the impression of physicality as if it were molded in the body. You cannot become fully enlightened and return to Nirvana if you have *"Tinh"* and *"Khi,"* but not *"Than."* You cannot make a spiritual body for the return to Nirvana if you have "Than" but not *"Tinh"* or *"Khi."* For the spiritual body to be created and enlightenment to occur, one must have all three elements: *"Tinh," "Khi,"* and *"Than"* united.

"Tinh" and *"Khi"* are all materials and will interact with cosmic ether where there is electricity.

To reach the universe, the soul must be pure, advanced and therefore lighter than atmospheric air. It must also be as genuinely good as the Saints, Immortals and Buddhas in order to reach those levels. A pure *"Than"* is produced by a pure body.

Meat-eating creates difficulties for one practicing meditation, in as much as it prevents the practitioner from effectively resolving complications which arise from meditation.

Even if you have no such complications, an impure physical body will create an impure spiritual body, which cannot conduct electricity well. As a result, it will then be struck by lightning and be destroyed in the atmosphere. Even if the impure spiritual body is wise and remains on the earth to avoid the lightning, it will remain an Immortal and never proceed to Buddhahood.

This is why I recommend the practice of complete vegetarianism before attempting meditation.

Thursday July 22, 1926
(The 13th day of the 6th month of the year of the Yang Fire Tiger)

JADE EMPEROR OR CAO DAI TIEN ONG DAI BO TAT MA HA TAT
TEACHING THE GREAT WAY FOR THE SOUTHERN QUARTER.

Death has been considered as final by lay people because they are ignorant and do not understand religious teachings. Almost all human beings on this earth worship Satan. Satan is always allied with death and will therefore be destroyed and never know the eternal life. (Laughter) If I cannot save you in time, you will perish.

Satan is like a musty and rotten rice seed which can never grow, bloom and produce seeds.

The devout person, on the contrary, is like a good seed which, once sowed, will certainly grow, bloom produce fruits and multiply progressively. You must abandon your physical body for your spiritual seed to multiply. It is the principle of the Tao. With only My spirit, I have created Buddhas, Immortals, Saints, Genies and all human beings in this universe. Therefore you are Me, I am you.

The Buddhist called *Nhien Dang* the founder of Buddhism, and *Nhien Dang* was born in the *Hien Vien Huynh De* dynasty.

People called *Quan Am* the female Buddha, and she was the spirit of *Tu Hang Dao Nhan,* who was born in the *Thuong* dynasty.

People called Sakya Muni Buddha; Sakya Muni was born in the *Chau* dynasty.

People called Lao Tse the founder of Taoism: he was also born in the *Chau* dynasty.

People called Jesus the founder of Christianity: he was born in the *Han* dynasty.

Who created those founders?

The Cosmic Ether created only Me. So, who created these founders? It was Tao, or Me.
You must understand this. If I did not exist, there would be nothing in the universe. And if there were no Cosmic Ether, then I would not exist either.

Sunday, July 25th, 1926
The 16th day of the sixth month of the year of the Yang Fire Tiger

CAODAI

(Laughter)

T..., look! You don't look bad in wearing the religious costume? One day people will recognize and respect it. Child, have you thought of that? (Laughter)

The student priests help to solemnize not only séances, but all ceremonies. They are to dress neatly, two positioned in front and two in back, ensuring that the séance is pure and serene. I have told you that were the seance not solemn, I would not appear. You three remember!

Tr..., L..., K..., T..., listen! Each of you four has a great mission. You should realize that even governing a country is easier than taming a cruel person. And your responsibility in this time of the 3rd spiritual amnesty is to save all humanity on all five continents. What a great mission! Your personality and your virtue should be commensurate with your responsibility. You are the example for all humanity. You have to develop yourselves spiritually to be worthy.

You have earned such a happy blessing because you are learning from Me. What happens if you do not listen and obey?

If you do not succeed in spiritual development, how can you expect to become Immortals and Buddhas?

Ngoc Dan (Giong Ong To)
Friday, July 30th, 1926 (the 21st day of the sixth month of the year of the Yang Fire Tiger)

JADE EMPEROR OR CAO DAI TIEN ONG DAI BO TAT MA HA TAT - TEACHING THE GREAT WAY FOR THE SOUTHERN QUARTER
DO NOT BE OBSCENE

Why is obscenity a severe crime? Ordinary people see the physical body as a single unit. In reality, it is a mass of innumerable living parts. These living parts are assembled to form a body with a divine personality. This body is nourished with other living beings such as vegetables, plants, fruits, rice--all of which are fresh and contain vital matter (because all these foods are living beings). If these foods did not contain fresh, vital matter, they would certainly simply wither and die. Thus, you would never eat things whose nutrients are already wasted. Cooking simply disinfects foods. The nutritional energy of these foods does not die after being cooked. Foods are then transformed in your gastrointestinal system into *"Khi"* (vital energy), and then into blood. Of course, you all know that there is spiritual energy in *"Khi"* and in blood. It is transformed into a human body as a result of the cycle of death and birth. Therefore, even a drop of blood has a certain amount of spiritual energy. Since sexual *"Tinh"* (life matter) is composed partly of blood and partly of "Khi," excessive sexual activity thus causes an unnecessary waste of *Tinh* and therefore of spiritual energy. After your death, you will be confronted with and judged by this spiritual energy, and the manner in which you wasted it, at the *"Nghiet Canh Dai."*** You will not be able to deny how you wasted your spirit. So, you should observe this precept closely. I take My leave.

Notes of the translator: * Foods change only in form during the process of digestion and absorption. Foods do not die after being cooked or digested because they constitute elements comprised of atoms. Atoms are not destroyed--they only change their arrangement, form and purpose.

** *"Nghiet Canh Dai"* is a place in the spiritual world where the spirits, after the death of their physical body, will see all the good and bad deeds that they has done during their physical lifetime.

Wednesday, 4 August 1926.
The 5th day of the 6th month of the year of the Yang Fire Tiger.

JADE EMPEROR, OR CAODAI TIEN ONG DAI BO TAT MA HA TAT, TEACHING THE GREAT WAY FOR THE SOUTHERN QUARTER.

Listen disciples!

Your physical eyes cannot distinguish the true and the false: I have therefore arranged many challenges everywhere in this world for reincarnated Saints, Immortals, and Buddhas. If ordinary people knew the miraculous system of God, they would not dare commit crimes, and with self cultivation, could even become enlightened and reach the positions of the Saints, Immortals, and Buddhas. For the incarnated Saints, Immortals, and Buddhas, these challenges are not difficult because they always follow God's laws. I have been telling you that this world is a school with many challenges; the only way for you to reach Nirvana is to pass these challenges. Should you desire this, you must cultivate your spiritual self and then you may even be able to teach and save millions of other living beings who are still immersed in this ocean of sufferance.
Now, although you have not seen the miracles which I have Myself described to you, you must trust my words, because if you wait until you leave this world to see the miracles, it will be too late for you.
Obey.

Saturday, August 7th, 1926

The 29th of the sixth month of the year of the Yang Fire Tiger

CAODAI

Greetings to all children!

Listen, children!

All the bad things on this earth are just tactics of the Demons to try to stop you on your Holy way. I ordered them to use all Evil tricks to challenge you. I have told you that I had left wild beasts living among you to devour you at any opportunity. However, I have also given you an armor to protect you, which is your virtue and which the beasts can never see. I encourage you to keep this armor until the day you come back to see Me. Your virtue, as well as the Tao, are extremely useful to you--like the armor to your body. If you abandon the armor, you are exposed to harm, and if you abandon the Tao, you will be possessed by Evils. Don't worry. When the Tao is opened, it also releases Evils at the same time. You have to try with all your heart to take care of yourself, not only your own selves, but all My disciples. I predict that among My chosen disciples, only half of them will succeed. The other half will be seduced by Evils, because I have allowed them to use My name to seduce you. (Laughter)

As many disciples I have sent, are lost. Don't be so sad. It is the divine mechanism. It is natural that among innumerable candidates, only a few may succeed at the examination. You have to try to elevate the faith of the disciples every day; this would be your first service credit.

August 9, 1926
The first day of the seventh month of the Year of the Fire Tiger

JADE EMPEROR, or CAO DAI TIEN ONG DAI BO TAT MA HA TAT, TEACHING THE GREAT WAY FOR THE SOUTHERN QUARTER

First Contact:
My greetings to you all.
Tho, you and your younger brothers must go to Can Giuoc to avert the evil that will otherwise surely befall My disciples there. *Quan Thanh (Guan Sheng Di Jun)* and *Quan Am (Kuan Yin Bodhisattava)* await you: Go immediately. Trung must attend to an emergency in his family, and so will not be joining you. (Tho, Hau, Nghia, Trang, Cu, Tac, and Sang arrived at Can Giuoc at 1:30 p.m. Seeing nothing amiss, they did not attempt to contact the Supreme Being until 3:00 p.m.)

Second Contact: Children, are you still playing? I ordered you to come here for an important matter and you keep delaying. Do you dare act against My will?
Tho: "I pray you to mercifully excuse us." It wasn't your fault, Tho. You should be in deep meditation in order to receive My instructions tonight. Tuong, call all My disciples right away.

Third Contact: My greetings to all My disciples. Listen: Tuong, do you not know what day is today? You have caused a stir among the Genies, Saints, Immortals and Buddhas.
Demons have come to the White Pearl Palace asking the right to challenge you both physically and spiritually. I did not allow the physical challenge. They even planned to summon the demons of the 36 caverns to harm you. I have

summoned *Quan Thanh* and *Quan Am* to protect you. However, most of you have not taken the oaths, and so they did not want to accept you. I therefore have ordered you to assemble here together to set up a ceremony for taking the oaths and for the celestial appointment of Tuong, Kim, and Tho. You must all be present here tonight.

Fourth Contact (midnight):
In this third revelation of the Great Way, Quan Am represents the Buddhas, Ly Thai Bach represents the Immortals, and Quan Thanh De Quan represents the Saints. Those three Lords will witness your ceremony. You will set up the altar of the Five Thunder Lords as I instructed before. Place *Kim Quang Tien* charms and also *Giang Ma Xu* charms on the *Ho Phap* altar. Cu shall hold the incense sticks for Me to summon the Five Thunder Lords. He will then join Tac and Sang at the *Ho Phap* altar, with all the other mediums in attendance. Ask Tuong, Kim, and Tho to say the oaths as before. All disciples must say the oaths as in the ceremony of celestial appointment. Remember to ask them to meditate--after all, they are being witnessed by Genies, Saints, Immortals and Buddhas.
Now hear your baptismal names:
"The Third Revelation of the Thanh Dao (pure Way) will endure seven hundred thousand years.
It endures as long as the earth, and will bloom as well as Heaven.
Human beings' *"khi"* (Chi) shall return to *Hu Vo* (the Cosmic Void),
Shining the way to Nirvana."
THANH is your baptismal name.

Thus: Tuong shall be henceforth Thuong* Tuong Thanh, Kim shall be henceforth Thuong* Kim Thanh, and Tho shall be henceforth Thai* Tho Thanh.
These are your names for saying the oaths.

Fifth Contact (1:30 a.m.)
Tuong, where are the four *Le Sanh* (Student Priests)?
Arrange the ceremony and I will summon Genies, Saints, Immortals and Buddhas as witnesses.

Sixth Contact (3:00 a.m.):
Lich, many disciples are missing.
Tomorrow, you must arrange a ceremony at Trung's house in Cho Lon so that all my disciples may say the oaths.
Holy Messages from Ly Thai Bach:
Thai Thuong (Lao Tzu's previous incarnation) did not say anything, but created the Tao
And looked after all human beings from the white cloud.
Since Man is part of God's spirit and has reincarnated into this world, he must cultivate himself.
I will help you to reach enlightenment.

Holy Message from Quan Am:
An enlightened being, I guard the gate of the Tao at the South Sea,
And often guide spirits away from Hell.
From my lotus throne, I always care about
And guide the people of this world to the Tao.

Holy Message from Quan Thanh:

I was a general of the Han Dynasty,
In which people preferred materialism over divine virtue.
By remaining loyal to the King,
I acquired a divine position with a red face and dressed in blue.

*Thai, Thuong and Ngoc denote Buddhist, Taoist, and Confucian Branches, respectively.

Vinh Nguyen Tu (Can Giuoc)
Saturday 21-8-1926
The 14th day of the 7th month of the year of the Yang Fire Tiger

JADE EMPEROR, or CAO DAI
TEACHING THE GREAT WAY FOR THE SOUTHERN QUARTER

Lich! Invite all Minh Duong disciples to listen to Me. (Laughter.)

Children! Do not think wrongly and assume that because you are of different sects that you belong to different religions. Let Me try to explain.

Although the doctrine of the Tao is old, it was always genuine and true, and the Tao has been unchanged since its closure. People become enlightened in accordance with their virtues and merits. Because *Ngoc Hu Cung* (Invisible Jade Palace) and *Loi Am Tu* (Thunderous Temple) rejected the guidelines for self-cultivation, only a few among many who were practicing the Tao have become enlightened.

Just look back in history; over a span of 2000 years in Asia, how many have become enlightened? You may notice only one case, of Hue Mang Kim Tien.

Notes:
Minh Duong is the name of a CaoDai sect.
Ngoc Hu Cung (Invisible Jade Palace) is the divine celestial cabinet.
Loi Am Tu (Thunderous Temple) is the divine headquarters of the Buddha.
Hue Mang Kim Tien is the name of an Immortal.

Sunday 22-8-1926
The 15th day of the 7th month of the year of the Yang Fire Tiger

JADE EMPEROR, or CAO DAI
TEACHING THE GREAT WAY FOR THE SOUTHERN QUARTER

Đ., listen:
Since *Bach Ngoc Kinh* (White Jade Palace) and *Loi Am Tu* (Thunderous Temple) established the "Third Universal Salvation," demons began interfering with the Tao; they have even used My name--but they have not yet dared to sit upon My throne.

They have seen My miraculous manifestations, and have tried imitating the miraculous mechanism by creating 36 caves after the fashion of the 36 heavens. They have used the names of all Genies, Saints, Immortals, and Buddhas in order to cement their unorthodox system.

You cannot fathom how dire is the crime of using Buddhas' and God's name for financial gain. Do you understand?

Your crimes would be punished in Hell. You must repent for these deeds so that I may redeem you at last. Guide humanity in order to repay your offenses. Obey!

Notes: Bach Ngoc Kinh (The white Jade Palace): the Palace of the Supreme Being.

Friday, August 27, 1926
The 22th day of the 7th month of the ear of the Yang Fire Tiger

JADE EMPEROR, or CAO DAI TIEN ONG DAI BO TAT MA HA TAT, TEACHING THE GREAT WAY FOR THE SOUTHERN QUARTER

Disciples, listen!
There should be 36 Saints for each of the three branches. At present, we have only eight or nine. The Hierarchy of the White Pearl Palace will organize the earthly positions. Lich, Trung, and Minh are the heads of the three branches, and represent Me to guide and teach you. Trang, Ky, and Kinh shall be renamed: Trang Thanh, Ky Thanh, and Kinh Thanh. Whomever you have brought to the faith has become part of your family. When you return to the White Pearl Palace, you will therefore have your own family; if you have not brought any one, you will return without that family. Those disciples who have committed themselves with the oath will be rewarded or chastised according to their accomplishments or their transgressions, but all must bring to the faith at least 12 people. Your earthly position will be equivalent to your divine position.
Each of you must in turn strive to reach your divine position by spiritual self-cultivation.
My only warning to you is not to think that a divine position is given to everyone at random or that everyone may enter the White Pearl Palace. Your names and positions are all already arranged in the divine list. You may attain earthly positions through bribery--not so the divine positions.
The faith would spread very quickly if that were possible, but each of you already has your own position that I cannot grant to anyone else unless you expressly refuse it.
Trang, I congratulate you.
Kinh, I also congratulate you.

Ban, I love you.
Tuong, I rely on you.
Ta, I leave human suffering in your care. I will even use your own house as a temple.
Hoc, obey your elder brother in the accomplishment of your mission.
Huong, try your best--I will help you.
Truoc, do not be so confused.
Nghia, I will use you.
Duc, you are to spread the faith all the way to the center.
Tràng, remember your chastisement. You must all cultivate your virtue and spread the faith quickly. You are all Me. To despise each other is the same as despising me, and that is hard. You must teach everyone, whether or not they listen to you.
If they understand My teachings through you and come back to the Great Way, they will be saved; otherwise, they will be lost.
This faith is very precious: It is not a merchandise for you to sell, so do not be discouraged.
I bless you, daughters. You must do your best to accomplish your duty.
I bless each of you.

Saturday, September 11, 1926
The fifth day of the eighth month of the Year of the Yang Fire Tiger

JADE EMPEROR, or CAO DAI TIEN ONG DAI BO TAT MA HA TAT, TEACHING THE GREAT WAY FOR THE SOUTHERN QUARTER

My greetings to all disciples.
Listen, children!
Consider Me: I am the Supreme Being, and yet I humble Myself--I condescend to your level to rescue you. I even refer to Myself as Tien Ong, and Bo Tat, the lowest ranks in Taoism and Buddhism, respectively. One would think that I would elevate Myself to the highest possible position--however, I do not do so (many of the disciples thought I had low self-esteem! (divine smile).
However, you have the responsibility to be modest. You must follow my example and humble yourselves so that you may save people. I said, when I founded this Holy Way, that I came to save guilty people. If there were no guilt in the world, I would not need to descend among you.
Thus, you have the responsibility to endeavor to save guilty people. This would please me the most.
Luu and Hieu must form a group of 36 young girls to chant the prayers in the major ceremonies. Cu, Tac, Sang and Phu will do the same for the young boys (Cu, you and Phu should remember to keep practicing your music!).

Friday, September 17, 1926
The 12th day of the 8th month of the year of the Yang Fire Tiger

JADE EMPEROR, or CAO DAI TIEN ONG DAI BO TAT MA HA TAT, TEACHING THE GREAT WAY FOR THE SOUTHERN QUARTER

Kiet, you are to help Tho in the construction of the temple. You are assigned the task of making seven thrones: a large throne for the *Giao Tong,* three for the three *Chuong Phap* (Censor Cardinals), and three for the three *Dau Su* Cardinals). Special attention is to be made in the creation of the throne of the *Giao Tong.* It must include four carved sacred animals at the arm rests: two dragons for those of the *Giao Tong,* two phoenixes for that of the *Chuong Phap,* and two unicorns for that of the *Dau Su.* Obey my instructions!

Binh, you are assigned to make a universal globe. Do you not know what that is? .... (Laughter).... It is a globe like the earth, understand? The diameter is 3.3 m. It is rather large because the miraculous mechanism of creation is represented in it. Paint it azure, draw the North Star and other stars on the globe. The thirty six heavens and the four great dimensions are not stars. Only 72 earths and three thousand worlds are considered stars, which make three thousand and seventy two stars in total. You must represent that number. Look in the Western books on Astronomy and imitate the pictures of the stars. For the North Star, you are to draw both the Ursa Major and Ursa Minor. Above the North Star is the Divine Eye. Understand? Theoretically, the globe should be in crystal, in which there is an eternal light, the precious vital principle for humanity and the universe. However, this must be completed by the time of the convention.

Obey my commands!

Regarding the statues of Buddhas, Immortals, Saints, and Angels, you may arrange them below the globe. Understand?

Saturday, September 18, 1926
The 13th day of the 8th month of the year of the Yang Fire Tiger

JADE EMPEROR, or CAO DAI TIEN ONG DAI BO TAT MA HA TAT, TEACHING THE GREAT WAY FOR THE SOUTHERN QUARTER

Your Master will now discuss some issues with His disciples. Guests are excused until further notice.

Children! I have founded the holy temple, which is your common house of prayer.

Understand also that I have united the three faiths and created the New Codes. There will be a convention of the three faiths on the fifteenth day of the tenth month at the temple. Remember this!

The rituals for the third salvation will be established at that time. Is this clear?

The purpose of uniting the three faiths is to bring all My children together in one family, of which I am the father. Please understand!

From now on in this country of the South, there will be only one true faith, which is the one that I have founded for you and which is called the national faith. Understand: You must, with all your heart and mind, obey it!

From this point forward, you must all work harder. I will give each of you an assignment. Irresponsibility, jealousy, competition, and divisiveness will be the great transgressions. Obey me! All else will stop for the convention.

Wednesday, September 22, 1926
The 15th day of the 8th month of the year of the Yang Fire Tiger

YOUR MASTER

Children

Trung, don't you know how much I love humanity? All difficulties come from the Karma of living beings. It is difficult to purify your body of the stain of all accumulated sins with only a cup of water. Humanity has been sinning for more than ten thousand years, so that one year of spiritual cultivation is certainly not long enough to make you completely pure and good.

Demons have managed to circumvent even My divine will, by trying to harm you. Poor children, struggling between Me and the Demons!

I teach you one thing: you must follow Me to defend yourself. You are obligated to defend when they attack. You must be stronger to defeat them. If you can withstand their attacks, the Tao will succeed. If you fall, the Tao will fail. It is your responsibility!

Having an unfathomable power in My grasp, I can destroy them completely in the blink of an eye, but I would not do so, because this would violate My ordering of divine justice. This struggle is also an excellent means to establish your own service credits.

Trung, Lich, you must gather disciples, draft the declaration of the faith, and then submit it to Me for correction. Obey me!

Wednesday, September 29, 1926
The 23rd of the 8th month of the year of the Yang Fire Tiger

JADE EMPEROR, or CAO DAI TIEN ONG DAI BO TAT MA HA TAT, TEACHING THE GREAT WAY FOR THE SOUTHERN QUARTER

Once I, your Master, speak to you, my disciples, you must understand and remember. Some of you went to spread the Tao but were very shy. Is this logical? Is this good, children? If an ignorant man tries to teach another such as he, they will both remain ignorant forever.

If they are criticized by the others as ignorant, they then become convinced that they are less intelligent than the others and question their faith. Is this logical? Is this good, children?

It is like a person in a house who sees another get wet in the rain: he jumps out to cover the wet person with his body, and gets wet himself, but then says to himself that the rain is too cold. Is he not stupid?

I have seen many disciples, who, while trying to teach people, have low self esteem, and are timid and shy. Is this not wrong?

Yes. They lacked personality. When you teach people out of love and justice, you value yourself highly. Why, then, should you be ashamed?

You must cultivate yourself spiritually, so that your personality and attitude are quite different than ordinary people so that you may approach the positions of Immortals and Buddhas.

It is like a child who is insulted, and who, afraid of being dishonored, returns insult with insult. This only dishonors him more than remaining quiet.

I have seen many of you who, not understanding the truth, criticized the faith itself when they were criticized. Is this not wrong? I have seen many of such a person among you.

I have told you repeatedly that your teacher is God, and you just need to have faith in Him only. Obey!

The divine positions in the White Pearl Palace are not for cruel and hostile persons. It is certainly strange to see many of them try to attain those positions by force. You need not do that, because although you look weak and gentle, you actually are strong. You look small, but you are in fact powerful. You look humiliated, but in reality you have a quiet, bold dignity.

Vendredi, 1 Octobre 1926

Ngọc-Hoàng Thượng-Đế Viết Cao-Đài
Tiên Ông Đại Bồ-Tát Ma-Ha-Tát
Giáo Đạo Nam Phương
DIEU TOUT-PUISSANT

G........

Vos deux époux trouvent bizarre que je vienne en cette façon. Savez-vous que le monde est à ce jour tellement méchant que l'ère de destruction approche. L'humanité s'entretue. Bien mal servie par la science, elle provoque la dissenssion et la guerre. La saint doctorine du Christianisme ne sert qu'à envenimer l'ambition des forts contre les faibles, et arme les premiers contre les derniers.

Il faut une nouvelle doctrine capable de maintenir l'humanité dans l'amour des créatures.

Seule la nation annamite conserve religieusement le culte millénaire des morts; quoique cette nation ne connaisse depuis sa création que la servitude, elle reste telle que je le désire...

Friday, October 1, 1926

JADE EMPEROR, or CAO DAI TIEN ONG DAI BO TAT MA HA TAT, TEACHING THE GREAT WAY FOR THE SOUTHERN QUARTER

ALMIGHTY GOD

G...
You two, husband and wife, find it strange that I would come in this way [by spiritism]. Know, then, that the world is so wicked today that the era of destruction approaches. Science has badly served the world, provoking (causing) disharmony and war. The holy teaching of Christianity has only served to inflame (increase) the ambitions of the strong against the weak, and to arm the first against the last.

There must be a new teaching capable of holding Mankind in the love of all creation.

Only the Vietnamese nation has religiously conserved the thousand-year-old cult of the dead; although this nation has known nothing but slavery since its inception, it remains as I desire it to remain...

Monday October 4, 1926
The 27th of the 8th month of the year of the Yang Fire Tiger

YOUR MASTER:

Listen male disciples! Confucius had three thousand disciples, but among them there were only 72 gentlemen.
Lao Tse had only one disciple, Nguon Thi. Jesus had 12 disciples, but when he was arrested the only disciple remaining faithful to him was Peter. Sakya Muni had four disciples, and yet three left, leaving only one.
Now, in coming to earth I have created for you one position of Buddha, three positions of Immortals, 36 positions of Saints, 72 positions of sages, and three thousand positions of disciples. You should understand that there has never been anything like that before.
In the White Pearl Palace, more than sixty years ago, Genies, Saints, Immortals, and Buddhas, volunteered to incarnate in order to save human beings from my wrath; and now they have committed more crimes than ordinary humans! Do you know why? In the past, you honored three faiths, and now you have a fourth, CaoDai. Have you ever known any other country to be blessed in this way?
The secular positions correspond to the sacred. Theoretically, according to your current virtues and personality, you deserve to be punished rather than rewarded with such possibilities. But because I love you, I allowed you to have them. And now a terrible thing has happened, such that even the Divine Emperor of the Great Net would have difficulty to return to his/her divine original position without a great deal of spiritual development while on this earth. Obey, children!

October 12, 1926
YOUR MASTER:

Children!
Why do I like you to dress in plain clothes?

Because plain clothes are an example of virtue. It represents frugality, one of the best virtues on this earth, because pride and vanity are a waste of your blessings.

Phuoc Linh Temple, the 15th day of the 9th month of the year of the Yang Fire Tiger
Sunday October 24, 1926

SAKYA MUNI BUDDHA: or CAO DAI TIEN ONG DAI BO TAT MA HA TAT, TEACHING THE GREAT WAY FOR THE SOUTHERN QUARTER

I should explain, because you have not had the New Codes.
Since you now have the Divine Eye, the statue of the Jade Emperor has become meaningless. I will now explain to you why, from the time of the first Buddhist Patriarch until the time of the sixth, people have worshipped Me at the most prominent place, the highest position. This is because it was I who created the universe. It was also I who created Immortals and Buddhas: I have said that with only My spirit I have created the universe and human beings. I am Buddhas, and Buddhas are Me.
You children are Buddhas, and Buddhas are you.
I exist so that you may exist, and so that Angels, Saints, Immortals, and Buddhas may exist.
I have used the eight trigrams to create the universe, which is called *Phap* (Dharma). From *Phap,* I then created ten thousand things and human beings, which are called Tang (humanity).
I am Buddha, the Master of *Phap* and *Tang,* who created faiths to lead you back to be united with Me.
After the creation of the universe, I founded the way of Buddhas first, then the way of Immortals, then the way for humanity. Now, at the end of the last era, the faiths will return to the beginning, so that when the faiths are reunified, one would see them in the reverse order of their establishment on earth: the way for humanity first, then the way of Immortals, then the way of Buddhas last.

In such a way, one would see Me behind the Buddhas, Immortals, Saints, and Angels, as if I were escorting them back to the cosmic ether, the nothingness, or Nirvana.

Regarding the offerings, wine represents *Khi* (chi), flowers *Tinh* (sperm, reproductive cells, or physical aspect), and tea *Than* (spirit).

The 15th day of the 9th month of the year of the Yang Fire Tiger
(Session organized at Mr. Ho Quang Chau, and Mrs. Phan Thi Lan's house)

JADE EMPEROR, or CAO DAI TIEN ONG DAI BO TAT MA HA TAT, TEACHING THE GREAT WAY FOR THE SOUTHERN QUARTER

Greetings to all disciples, and all attendants.
Chau, listen:
From this time forward, your country will not be thrice divided.
I hereby unite all of you, my children, into one family.
Both South and North will go abroad,
Holding Me in their hearts as the one Truth.
I give you the responsibility of spreading the Tao to central Vietnam. You must strive to cultivate yourselves spiritually. Tho, open widely the temple to all without discrimination. Everyone is My child. Encourage all to join the Tao.

Re-evocation
Your Master, children.
Dao Quang, open the prayer session for them. Show them the method of worshipping Me, according to the New Codes. They need not say the oath, because they are already My disciples. (divine laughter) I do not know when you all will understand who your Master is. What a tragedy! What a pity! Trung, so much the worse for them. They thought that you are simply acting politically. Because you insist you were not doing so, I believe you. However, you must understand that politics and the Tao can never work together. I say little, but you understand much.

Mercredi 27 Octobre 1926
17 tháng 9 năm Bính Dần

Ngọc-Hoàng Thượng-Đế Viết Cao-Đài
Tiên Ông Đại Bồ-Tát Ma-Ha-Tát
Giáo Đạo Nam Phương

L'humanité souffre de toutes sortes de vicissitudes. J'ai envoyé Allan Kardec; j'ai envoyé Flammarion comme j'ai envoyé Elie et Saint-Jean-Baptiste, précurseurs de l'avènement de Jésus Christ; l'un est persécuté, et l'autre tué. Et par qui? Par l'humanité. Mon fils est aussi tué par vous; vous ne le vénérez qu'en Esprit et non en Sainteté.

Je voulais causer avec vous en une seule fois au temps de Moise sur le Mont-Sinai, vous ne pouviez me comprendre. La promesse que j'ai faite à vos ancêtres pour votre rédemption, la venue du Christ est prédite; vous ne voulez pas en tenir compte. Il faut que je me serve moi-même maintenant d'un moyen plus spirituel pour vous convaincre. Vous ne pourrez pas nier devant le Grand-Jugement-Général que je ne sauve pas l'humanité par tous moyens plausibles. Quelque indulgent que je sois, je ne pourrai effacer tous vos péchés depuis votre création. Le monde est dès maintenant dans les ténèbres. La vertu de Dieu est détruite; la haine universelle s'envenime; la guerre mondiale est inévitable.

La race française et la race annamite sont mes deux bénites.

Je voudrais que vous soyez unis pour toujours. La nouvelle doctrine que j'enseigne a pour but de vous mettre dans une communauté d'intérêt et de vie. Soyez donc unis par ma volonté et préchez au monde la paix et la concorde.

En voilà assez pour vous ce soir.

Wednesday, October 27, 1926
Month 9, Day 17, Year of the Yang Fire Tiger

JADE EMPEROR, or CAO DAI TIEN ONG DAI BO TAT MA HA TAT, TEACHING THE GREAT WAY FOR THE SOUTHERN QUARTER

Humanity suffers from all sorts of trials and tribulations. I sent Allan Kardec, I sent Flammarion [19th Century astronomer and spiritist]--as I sent Elijah and Jesus Christ: one is persecuted, and the other killed. And by whom? By Mankind. You also killed my son; you, who venerate him only in spirit but not in holiness. Once, I desired to communicate with you on Mount Sinai during Moses time, but you could not understand Me. You did not take into consideration either the promise I made to your ancestors for your redemption or the prediction of the coming of the Christ. Now I must Myself provide a more spiritual means to convince you. You will not be able to deny before the Grand Inquisitor that I attempted to save Mankind by all means possible. How ever indulgent I may be, I will not be able to blot out all the sins you have committed since the creation of Mankind. The world is even now in shadow. The Virtue of God was wiped out; universal hate was inflamed; world war was inevitable. The French and the Vietnamese are my two blessed races. I would like you to be united forever. The new doctrine I teach has for a goal to place you both in a union of interest and life. Be then united by my will and preach peace and harmony to the world.
This is enough for you this evening.

28 Octobre 1926
18 tháng 9 năm Bính Dần
Ngọc-Hoàng Thượng-Đế Viết Cao-Đài
Giáo Đạo Nam Phương

DIEU TOUT-PUISSANT qui vient sous le nom de CAO-ĐAI pour dire la VÉRITÉ en Annam.

M. et V...

Venez après d'ici,

Croyez-vous qu'il est impossible à DIEU de faire ce qu'il veut faire?

M... - Tu es désigné par moi pour accomplir une tâche ingrate mais humanitaire. Tu relèves par tes nobles sentiments la décadence d'une race millénaire qui a sa civilisation.

Tu te sacrifies pour lui donner une vraie morale. Voilà une toute faite pour ton oeuvre. Lis toutes mes saintes paroles; cette doctrine sera universelle. Si l'humanité la pratique, ce sera la paix promise pour toutes les races. Tu feras connaitre à la France que l'Annam est digne d'elle.

Tu as assez pour ce soir.

October 28, 1926

JADE EMPEROR, ALIAS CAO-DAI, TEACHING THE GREAT WAY FOR THE SOUTHERN QUARTER

ALMIGHTY GOD, who comes under the name of Cao Dai to speak TRUTH in Vietnam.

M... and V...

Come near here. Do you believe that it is impossible for GOD to do as he wishes?

M. . . .--I designate you to perform a thankless, yet humane task. You are relieving by your noble sentiments the decadence of a thousand-year-old race that has its own civilization. You are sacrificing yourself to give it a true morality. Here is something ready-made for your work: Read all my holy words. This doctrine will be universal. If Mankind practices it, the peace promised to all races will indeed be realized. You will make France understand that Vietnam is worthy of her. That is enough for you this evening.

Dai Dan (Cho Lon), October 29, 1926

JADE EMPEROR, or CAO DAI TIEN ONG DAI BO TAT MA HA TAT, TEACHING THE GREAT WAY FOR THE SOUTHERN QUARTER

Greetings to all disciples, all attendants, and all beloved daughters.
Children, listen!
I must clarify Myself so that you will not be confused and blame Me. A gentle father would never abuse his children. I have come to guide each of you, so there is no reason to chase you away. I have witnessed with broken heart many challenges set up by the three Lords. I would not allow these three Lords to blame Me for being unjust, because I love you too much, especially Ly Thai Bach, who beseeched Me the most.
Quan Am (Kuan Yin Bodhisattava) and *Quan Thanh* (Guan Sheng Di Jun, Kuan Kung/Guan Gong) were even unable to defend you, particularly on that special day of the opening ceremony of the new temple. It was My fault that you failed. If I understood your faith, I would have accepted you the way you were. I had given you predictions through spiritual messages, but you did not listen to them, so all My words were useless, and you became impertinent to Superiors.
So from now on, Ly Thai Bach will administer justice (in rewarding and punishing). You will to pray to him. You did not listen to My teachings, and so now you must accept your punishment.
(D. Q. submitted his messages)
Divine laughter. D.Q.
All you disciples are so narrow minded. Whoever has the intention to divide is My enemy. Understand, child! I have

been telling you that you are to wait for My orders for anything. Did I allow you to baptize T.'s mother? T. had lost his faith because of your cunning. Do you understand? Was the money such a great temptation?

T.! Meditate on this! I need say nothing more!

Trung, Trang, Tuong, you three children remember what I told you! Understand?

Re-evocation.
LY THAI BACH

Greetings to disciples. Divine/Celestial appointees, please sit down!

From now on, the Master has given me the power of justice. You disciples must attempt to solidify the Tao according to the divine will, in order to progress spiritually. Do not be shy and confused, and waste all your hard work by going against the will of the Master who has been striving to save all living beings.

Creating a faith is a difficult process. It is difficult to be born at the time of the creation of the Tao. Discipline, justice, rewards and punishments are necessary. Reward is a method to encourage good accomplishment. Punishment is a method to correct evil.

Reward and punishment may not be literal. They may only be incomparable joy or sadness that no one can find on earth. Even if you repent for the sins you have already committed, you still may not be able to return to your divine position.

Many of you have worked hard to build the Tao, but are still greedy and pursuing secular ambitions and desires.

You may have accumulated many credits, but seem tired to continue the walk and become easily despondent when confronted with. What a pity!

You are so blessed to be guided and taught by the Supreme Being, and yet you do not try your best in your improvement, but instead compete with each other for material things. If there were no ultimate love from the Master, all your credits would be wasted.

From now on, I am guiding you step by step. Do your best to listen and do my will. With your accumulated credits and blessings, you can progress to higher positions. If you fail, you will go to Hell. It is difficult to know who will be blessed and who will not be blessed. Luck and misfortune. Who knows? However, I am not at fault.

Good bye!

November 1, 1926
The 26th day of the 9th month of the year of the Yang Fire Tiger
Minh Tan Session.

Thai Thuong Lao Quan

Attendants! Do you not know what era you are in? Do you repent?

The three faiths will end soon. You are blessed to be present at this time when the Tao is created. You will be guided by the Master. After this time, there will be no one else to save you. Spread the good news to all the people so that they have time to join us. Blame no one for being late.

V..., M..., D..., have you listened? It's time now to guide the people. Let Me, your Master, give you your assignments.

Te Thien Dai Thanh.

You male disciples should move back somewhat to allow space for the female disciples to kneel on the right side. Kha, I come here today because of your sincere respect. Female disciples also are sincere. I will teach them first so that they may retire earlier. Ngoc Tam and Ngoc Y, obey my orders. Ngoc Tam, you must be cooperative in this life, and you must be loyal to your husband. I have accepted Kha, your husband, into the Minh Tan (Minh Tan is a Chinese Buddhist sect); and you therefore belong to Minh Tan. And Ngoc Y, your in-laws are with Minh Tan, so you belong to Minh Tan, also. I have asked Le Son, the Holy Mother, to guide you. The Minh Tan Sect will establish its Female College in order to merge into the Female College of the Third Universal Salvation, but it must be done right away, otherwise it will be too late for universal salvation.

Female disciples! You may keep your personal appointments at your assigned places, or you may choose to follow Le Son, the Holy Mother. This is enough for female disciples. You would then await Le Son, the Holy Mother, for further teaching. Now let me teach the male disciples. Kha, do you remember what I taught? You are sick, but your sickness is from your anger, which stimulates your inner fire and spirit. If you can control your anger, you will improve. Vi, you must learn from your father in order to manage all his secular works from the family to the community, so that he may have more time for the Tao. Once one member of the family becomes enlightened, he/she may subsequently save his/her family for nine generations! Is this not a precious thing? You and your father must hurry to take the oath. Van, have you chosen a date for your gateway ceremony? The 12th day is good, but is so close to the convention. It should be done on the 6th day of the 10th month. All disciples who are to take the oath will be there. I have explained to you generally about your personal family business. Kha and your father, obey! Vi and your father, obey! I will teach you the principle of the Tao later. Now, it is time for Le Son, the Holy Mother, to teach the female disciples.

Le Son, the Holy Mother:

You female Vietnamese disciples should know that this salvation does not happen all the time but just at one particular time. Now that the Great Way is about to end, your Master has asked me to guide you, the Female College of the Minh Tan sect. You female disciples have been confined to home, reciting prayers, and have never met other disciples. According to your Master's wishes, I now establish the Female College of the Minh Tan Sect. Do you agree?
Express your own opinion for every one to hear.
After the establishment of the Female College of the Minh Tan Sect, you must submit to the declaration to the Third Universal Salvation. The male disciples will do the same.

Whoever has not taken the oath of the Third Universal Salvation must submit a request. I only mention this, but there is no obligation for any one to do so.

Muoi asked question.....

After taking the oath, you then request the prayer book and try to develop yourself spiritually at home. It is not a good tradition for women to be outside on the street. Any one is welcome to do differently, but for the Female College of Minh Tan, you must work on your spiritual development at home. At any time when there is a spiritual session, you may come to the temple to receive teachings, but otherwise, you must go home after the ceremony.

Now it is open for you to sign up for the Minh Tan Female College.

I have spoken.

On the 6th, there will be a gateway ceremony here for male disciples. Let female disciples aware of this date for their convenience.

Friday, November 12, 1926
O môn, the 8th day of the 10th month of the year of the Yang Fire Tiger

JADE EMPEROR, or CAO DAI TIEN ONG DAI BO TAT MA HA TAT, TEACHING THE GREAT WAY FOR THE SOUTHERN QUARTER

K., if you understood the miracle of reincarnation, which is not as you usually imagined, you would not be sad and blame Me, your Master. At the White Pearl Palace, you are all My children who are brothers and sisters.

You must reincarnate many times before you may attain Nirvana. A word said to each other is enough by itself for you to incarnate on earth to help each other. It is fate. Regarding the founding of the Tao, although it required only a year to form, it was the result of the works of Immortals and Buddhas for many years prior all over the five continents.

This is similar to Chau Cong, who promoted humanism before its founding, or Moses, Elias, Jeremiah, John the Baptist before the birth of Jesus, or Hong Quan Lao To, Lao Tse, Thong Thien Giao Chu before the birth of Nguon Thi of Taoism, or Nhien Dang Buddha, or Brahma before the birth of Sakya Muni.

Before the founding of CaoDai, Genies, Saints, Immortals, Buddhas had come to all countries to prepare the way.

Saturday, November 20, 1926
The 16th of the 10th month of the year of the Yang Fire Tiger
Tu Lâm Temple

JADE EMPEROR, or CAO DAI TIEN ONG DAI BO TAT MA HA TAT, TEACHING THE GREAT WAY FOR THE SOUTHERN QUARTER

The *Giao Tong* is your eldest brother, who represents Me, to guide you in your spiritual and temporal lives. He holds only the temporal power--not the spiritual one. He may communicate with the thirty six Heavens and the seventy two Earths to ask for the salvation of the followers' spirits. Please understand! Obey, disciples!

There are three *Chuong Phap* (Censor Cardinals), one for each of the three branches: Confucianism, Buddhism and Taoism. Although the rules of the three faiths seem different, they are all one to Me. The three *Chuong Phap* have the right to examine the religious codes before they are implemented, whether the proposed codes come from the *Giao Tong* or from the *Dau Su* (Cardinals). If the two parties (the Giao Tong and the Dau Su) disagree, these proposed codes should be sent to the *Ho Phap* (Law Protector), who will bring them to the *Hiep Thien Dai* (Heavenly Union Palace), where he will invoke Me for the modification of the codes, or he may change it himself. The three *Chuong Phap* therefore have the right to examine the prayer books before they are published. If they find any book dangerous to traditional morals, they will forbid its publication. All followers have to get together to support them. Each *Chuong Phap* has his own seal. The three seals must all be present on each code for it to be valid. All disciples obey!

The *Dau Su* (Cardinals) have the right to administer the religion, and have jurisdiction over the disciples, both spiritually and temporally. They have the right of to make new laws. However, any laws must be approved by the *Giao Tong*. The *Giao Tong* must examine them carefully to verify that the proposed laws would be useful to humanity and then must ask the *Chuong Phap* to examine the laws before approving them.

The *Dau Su* must respectfully obey the *Giao Tong's* orders. They may ask the *Giao Tong* to abolish any laws which could be contrary to the activities and interests of the followers.

I ask you to love and help them. Remember, if there is any issue important to humanity, you are to address it to them.

Although the three branches are different, they have the same importance. If all three *Dau Su* disagree on any law ordered by the *Giao Tong,* this law must be returned to the *Giao Tong,* who will submit it to the *Chuong Phap* for reexamination. Each *Dau Su* has his own seal. Any document must have all three seals of the *Dau Su* before implementation. Understand? All disciples obey!

There are thirty-six *Phoi Su* (Archbishops) for the three branches, twelve for each. Among them, there are three *Chanh Phoi Su* (Principal Archbishops). The *Chanh Phoi Su* have the *Dau Su's* authority, but do not have the right to request amendment or abolishment of laws. Understand? All disciples obey!

There are seventy-two *Giao Su* (Bishops) in total, twenty-four for each branch. They have jurisdiction over the spiritual and temporal education of the faithful. They take care of them as they would their brothers. They maintain all the registries of the faithful and provide help to them with weddings and funerals. In larger cities, the *Giao Su* have the right to preside over religious ceremonies, as do the *Dau Su* or the *Phoi Su.* They also have the right to request abolishment or modification of laws, which could be otherwise harmful to the faithful.

The *Giao Huu* (Priests) have the mission of propagating the faith. They have the right to request modification of the religious laws and to preside over religious ceremonies in the smaller cities. There are three thousand *Giao Huu,* one thousand for each branch. This number may not be increased or decreased.

The *Le Sanh* (Student-Priests) are chosen among the sub-dignitaries, who exhibit good character. They have the right to preside over the altar installation ceremony at a follower's home. Remember that I love the *Le Sanh.* Do not take advantage on them. To become dignitaries, one must first become a *Le Sanh,* except I specifically appoint dignitaries via séances. Understand? All disciples obey!

The *Dau Su* may only be promoted to the position of *Chuong Phap* by a special election held by all of them. The *Phoi Su* may only be promoted to the position of *Chuong Phap* by a special election held by all of them. The *Giao Su* may only be promoted to the position of *Phoi Su* by a special election by all of them. The *Giao Huu* may only be promoted to the position of *Giao Su* by a special election by all of them. The *Le Sanh* may only be promoted to the position of *Giao Huu* by a special election by all of them. Only the *Chuong Phap* and *Dau Su* may be candidates for the *Giao Tong* election. They are to be promoted to the *Giao Tong's* position by an election held by all the followers.

Everyone must obey these election regulations, except when it is instructed differently by Me through a spiritism séance.

All disciples obey!

I bless you all.

Tu Lam Temple, the 19 day of the 10th month of the year of the Yang Fire Tiger
Tuesday, November 23, 1926

YOUR MASTER:

Children, don't be annoyed; what happened at the temple is merely an obstacle of the Tao. I am sad. It is the divine way. I acknowledge your credits. I would like to strengthen the Tao by yielding to your wishes, which have affected me very much, on what has happened. I have been arranging the Tao according to your wishes. What happened at the temple was contrary to the Tao and due to the evil natures of many of you. Your high and noble natures would be a medium for Immortals and Saints; in like manner, your evil natures would be a medium for evil spirits. At any rate, believing in My help to found the Tao is enough. I can control evil spirits. Rely on Me and progress carefully. Do not hurry; but do not regress; you will be satisfied one day.

I bless you. I ascend.

Notes of the translator: A grand Opening ceremony of the Third Universal Salvation of the Great Way took place on November 20, 1926 at Tu Lam Temple. Because of lack of spiritual security, evil spirits came and disturbed the ceremony, leading to confusion, loss of faith, and the discouragement of many disciples.

Wednesday, November 24, 1926
The 20th day of the 10th month of the year of the Yang Fire Tiger

YOUR MASTER:

I am sad and heartbroken, thinking about the events at the temple recently, when evil spirits abused the temple.
What do you think?
You cannot understand the divine mechanism. It is the fate of the Tao. I am sad because many of you exaggerated and spoke ignorantly concerning what happened. I initially thought I should punish them severely, but I still have pity and mercy for them. Many disciples wanted to quit, leaving of their religious costumes, straw sandals, and religious turbans to return to their secular lives. This was merely an obstacle, a difficulty of the Tao! You became tired of your cultivation, because you still have many secular obligations and many desires for wealth and honor. You understand now why I am sad! But it was the divine way that no one can do anything about. I have endured many hardships because of you.
Since the creation of the universe, because I love you, I have endured miseries, imprisonment and worries in raising you and in establishing the Tao for you. You should think about it, repent and return to the right way.
Many times in the past, as soon as I tried to build the Tao for you, you ruined it all. I am sad. I bless you.
I ascend.

Re-evocation:

Children! Listen to Me, your Master.
This event has become a forum of discussion which is noisy enough to affect the Tao; one called it evil, others called it right. The discussion was totally useless: the celestial manual had clearly predicted this. Whoever was blessed, whoever

was unfortunate, whoever believed, whoever did not believe, no one could change the divine mechanism. The longer the path, the harder the walk; the higher the Tao, the brighter your credit.

Alas! I have been enduring many hardships for innocent children. I wanted to guide and to save all humanity from this ocean of suffering, but humanity is so soaked in secular seductions, their minds are so unstable, their patience before difficulties is so fragile, that they are prepared to regress as soon as they step on a spike on the road! I am so heartbroken to hold the miraculous divine mechanism and to watch what is occurring! You must think and manage yourself.

Dimanche 28 Novembre 1926
24 tháng 10 năm Bính Dần
Ngọc-Hoàng Thượng-Đế Viết Cao-Đài
Giáo Đạo Nam Phương

DIEU TOUT-PUISSANT qui vient sous le nom de CAO-ĐÀI pour dire la Vérité en Annam

L......

Une séance spécial n'est donné que rarement aux gens pour un voeu de quelque importance que ce soit; mais à toi dont je connais les sentiments d'humanité et l'esprit charitable, à toi je donne entière satisfaction.

En dehors de tes volontés religieuses, tu as l'intention de t'informer de cette nouvelle doctrine qui t'a été travestie par quelques uns de tes compatriotes sous une forme quelque peu malicieuse. Sur cette terre dont le peuple est si doux et paisible, je viens comme le Christ était venu parmi vous pour combattre l'hérésie et évangéliser le monde. Quelle que soit la race dont vous faites partie, enfants de la Terre, vous avez tous un même père, c'est Dieu qui préside à vos destinées. Pourquoi vous séparez vous à cause de divergences d'opinion religieuses, alors que tous, vous êtes appelés à souffrir et faire votre Purgatoire en ce monde?

Tu as déjà mis pied dans ce chemin qui conduit tout humain, vers l'heureux séjour qu'est le Nirvâna.

Tâche de continuer cette voie pour arriver à ton but.

De bons Esprit guideront tes pas. Tous tes voeux seront exaucés. C'est assez pour toi.

Au revoir.

Sunday November 28, 1926
The 26th day of the 10th month of the year of the Yang Fire Tiger

JADE EMPEROR, or CAO DAI TIEN ONG DAI BO TAT MA HA TAT, TEACHING THE GREAT WAY FOR THE SOUTHERN QUARTER

The Almighty God who comes under the name of CaoDai to teach the truth in Annam.
L....
A special séance is seldom granted to person with a wish of any importance; however to you whom I know the feelings of humanism and the compassionate heart, I would bring all satisfaction.
Outside of your religious will, you have the goal to inform yourself about that new doctrine which was revealed to you in a somewhat distorted and derisive way by some of your compatriots. On this earth with its people so sweet and peaceful, I come like the Christ had come among you to fight heresy and evangelize the world. Whichever race you belong to, children of the earth, you all have the same father, God who presides on your destiny. Why do you segregate from each other because of differences in religious opinions, while all of you are to suffer and to pay your karma on this world?
You have already place your step on this path which lead all humans to the happy stay which is Nirvana.
Try hard to continue on this path in order to reach your goal. Good spirits will guide your steps. All your wishes will be fulfilled. This is enough for you. Good bye.

Thursday, December 2, 1926
The 28th day of the 10th month of the year of the Yang Fire Tiger
TayNinh Holy temple

THAI BACH

Our Master orders me to come to improve the function of the temple.
From now on, you have to follow the rules of the temple:
No courting between males and females within the temple.
Males shall remain on the East side, females on the West, separately.
No courting; and there is to be no chatting in the sanctuary, except for husband and wife, or between brothers and sisters, or if there are two witnesses: one from the male side, one from the female side.
In the kitchen, males and females may work together in cooking, but when you serve meals, serve males and females separately.
Heed the rule.
Tho Thanh, you must post these rules at the temple. Obey.

Monday December 6, 1926
The 2nd day of the 11th month of the year of the Yang Fire Tiger

JADE EMPEROR, or CAO DAI TIEN ONG DAI BO TAT MA HA TAT, TEACHING THE GREAT WAY FOR THE SOUTHERN QUARTER

Greetings to all disciples, beloved daughters and guests. Listen.

I, out of great love and mercy, have founded the Third Universal Salvation of the Great Way based on love of life, with the purpose of raising the predestined spirits to higher dimensions, avoiding reincarnation, and bringing the virtuous to a more precious domain of freedom and repose than this poor, vile earthly world.

Alas! Many, many people partake in worldly happiness, while ignoring self-cultivation in the Tao which would lead them to enlightenment. They argue, criticize the Tao thinking that they are now in higher secular positions than other people, without knowing that only punishment awaits them in the next realm.

Whoever is blessed will be in a higher world; whoever is unfortunate will remain confused. The celestial laws have determined so. In the end, the more meritorious your life, to the better world of freedoms you shall be led.

It's a rare privilege to be living in the days of the founding of the Tao. It's even rarer to successfully walk the thorny path of Tao; it is like searching for pearls in the deep, dark forest. Yet it all depends on your state of mind: if you believe the way is smooth, it will be so. If you think it's difficult, it will likewise be so. Don't be led to confusion in walking the path of the Tao, or you shall too late awaken to your folly.

December 6, 1926

YOUR MASTER, children.

Children, listen:
The world has lost one of My disciples today, one of your co-disciples who has shared with you some responsibility in the founding of the Third Universal Salvation of the Great Way.
Tuong's death is his fate. He is blessed in returning to Me. Death sometimes causes joy and sometimes causes sorrow. People on this earth who know how to make themselves useful to their communities and who know how to self-cultivate, would consider death as just the end of a long journey Home and as the accomplishment of their duty and time to reap their reward. Although he has not been such a person, his virtue and his meritorious service in building the Great Way would lead him to an extraordinary celestial position. His spirit will first, however, have to appeal to the triune-faith court and wait for his destiny according to his past deeds. It was of My will in creating these rules for you to follow. You should understand.
Regarding his funeral, you should join together to accomplish your human duty toward him.
Trang, tell Trung, Tho, Tuong, Hoa and other celestial appointees to escort him to his place of eternal rest. This act manifests the dignity of a virtuous person. Whoever is busy would be excused. You should also hurry to organize the ceremony to make it brilliant. The prayers should be the same as with the funeral of Hau's mother, except just a minor difference.

Session at Cho Lon, December 13, 1926
YOUR MASTER, children.

It's not an insignificant bit of business by which I founded the genuine faith for Vietnam. If you know that the Tao is extraordinarily precious, you should give utmost attention to its care; if you wait for its ultimate success in order to recognize the celestial mechanism at work, even if you would like to contribute then, you would not rate so much merit as if you contributed now, at the time of its arduous birth. I implore you, therefore, to endeavor practice the Way (Tao) with all sincerity. Practicing the Tao is not just an exercise of the tongue.

I have also seen that many of you adhere to the Tao for some evil motive. Because of love of humanity, and because I want to save humanity, I have endured cruel people in order to give them time to repent, to return to the right path to live a blessed life in the future; those who do not repent are lost and cannot be saved. If you wait until your last breath to acknowledge the sublime and the evil, it would be too late. You have to regularly play judge upon oneself.

Heed me!

Mercredi 15 Décembre 1926
11 tháng 11 năm Bính Dần

Thái-Bạch

Hỉ chư Đạo hữu Chư Nhu, Chư Tín Nữ

Chỉnh đàn cho nghiêm đặng Thầy ngự.

Qu'on dise à ces Français, qu'ici est une maison de prières qu'il ne faut pas qu'il la considèrent comme une curiosité.

Ngọc-Hoàng Thượng-Đế Viết Cao-Đài
Giáo Đạo Nam Phương

M....., Debout et lis.

Toute chose vient à son heure.

Tu as vu et su ce que la plupart de tes compatriotes cherchent à voir et à savoir. Ce n'est qu'à la suite de la conclusion des recherches spirites que j'enseigne cette nouvelle doctrine.

N'ai-je pas prédit que le spiritisme est une religion d'avenir? Tu as naturellement l'intention de créer en ce pays, une relation morale des deux races française et annamite appelées à vivre ensemble par ma volonté dans une communauté de vie et d'intérets. Tu seras satisfait par une vie d'un homme de bien. Tes voeux seront exaucés. Tu seras plus tard un de mes fervents disciples pour prêcher au monde la paix et la concorde.

L'équipe française sera bientôt créé.

Tu sera force de revenir en France en 1928, pour soutenir cette doctrine au Congrès Universel. Tu seras grand et puissant pas volonté.

Au revoir. c'est assez pour toi.

The Holy See of Tay Ninh, December 15, 1926.
(the 11th day of the 11th month of the year Binh-Dan)

THAI-BACH*

Greetings, my brothers.

Prepare to respectfully receive Our Divine Master,
Tell to these French present that this is a house of prayer and must not be considered merely a curiosity.

JADE EMPEROR, or CAO DAI,
TEACHING THE GREAT WAY FOR THE
SOUTHERN QUARTER

MONET, arise and read.
All things come in their time.
You have seen most of what your compatriots wish to see and know. This new doctrine that I teach is the result of spiritual studies.
Have I not predicted that spiritism is a religion of the future? You naturally wish to create in this country a moral relationship between the two races, French and Vietnamese, who have been called to live together, by My will, in a commonality of life and interests. You will be satisfied by living a gentlemanly life. Your prayers will be heard. You will later be one of my most devoted disciples in preaching peace and harmony to the world.
The French team will be created soon.
You will be forced to return to France in 1928, to defend this teaching before the Universal Congress. You will be big and strong by My will.
Goodbye, this is enough for you.

---

* THAI-BACH is the Spiritual Giao Tong (Pope) of CaoDai.

Vendredi 17 Décembre 1926
13 tháng 11 năm Bính Dần

Thái-Bạch

M.D... est prié d'attendre la venu du Divin-Maitre

Ngọc-Hoàng Thượng-Đế Viết Cao-Đài
Giáo Đạo Nam Phương

DIEU TOUT-PUISSANT qui vent sous le nom de CAO-ĐAI pour enseigner la Vérité en Annam.

D....., Debout et lis.

Je tiens à te dire que rien ne se crée et n'existe sur se globe sans ma volonté. De pauvres esprits prétendent qu'ils sont dans le secret de Dieu. Or, je ne donne à nul humain ici-bas d'en faire la révélation. Pour venir à moi, il faut des prières. Je ne néglige pas à me manifester quand ces prières sont sincères. Il suffit, pour vous convaincre que je suis bien Jéhovah des Hébreux, Le Dieu des Armées des Israélites, le Dieu inconnu des Juifs et le vrai Père de Jésus-Christ, de me prier par le prête-nom CAO-ĐAI pour que vos voeux soient exaucés. Tu viens à moi avec un sentiment sincère pour bien faire aux peuples soumis qui te sont confiés. Je te prie alors de propager cette doctrine à tous tes protégés. C'est la seule qui maintient l'humanité dans l'amour des créature et vous apporte une paix durable.

Friday, December 17th, 1926
The 13th day of the 11th month of the year of the Yang Fire Tiger.

Thai Bach.

M. Đ..., you are requested to attend the arrival of the Divine Master.

JADE EMPEROR, or CAO DAI, TEACHING THE GREAT WAY FOR THE SOUTHERN QUARTER

Almighty God, who comes under the name of CaoDai to teach the truth in Annam*.
D..., arise and read.
I declare unto you that nothing is created nor exists on this Earth against My will. Some poor spirits claimed that they possess the secrets of God. But I have not given to any human here the mission to reveal such. To reach Me you are only to pray; I do not fail to manifest when those prayers are sincere. Realize that I am Jehovah of the Hebrew, God of the Israelites, the God of unspoken name to the Jews, and the Father spoke of by Christ; if you pray to me in the name of CaoDai, your prayers will be heard. Come to Me sincerely and do good unto your brothers, whom I have entrusted to you. And I ask you to spread this teaching to all of those under your watch and care. It is the only message which can raise humanity to abiding love and bring a lasting peace.

Annam is the old name of Vietnam.

Sunday, December 19, 1926
Day 15, Month 11, Year of the Fire Tiger

JADE EMPEROR, or CAO DAI TIEN ONG DAI BO TAT MA HA TAT, TEACHING THE GREAT WAY FOR THE SOUTHERN QUARTER

Listen, children:

One thing remains you have not learned (and so do not know or recognize), and that is the true value of the Great Way. It is so great that you should indeed be concerned about improving your conscience and spiritually developing your emotions. You were born here on this earth: You live and suffer here, and you will also die here.
Do you know what will happen to you after your death?
Do you know where you will go?
None of you understands this miraculous, mystic mechanism. I will now explain: Throughout many thousands of years, all beings are transformed through the reincarnation cycle from minerals to plants to animals--finally reaching the stage of human beings. Human beings on this earth are themselves divided into different classes. For example, the class of "Emperor," as you understand it, on this earth (the 68th world*) is not even as worthy as the lowest class on the lower, 67th world. The value of worlds increases as their assigned number decreases, from the 3,000th world to the first, then through the 72 earths, then through the four great ethereal continents and then finally through the 36 heavens. Human beings must persevere in cultivating themselves to reach the pinnacle, the *"Bach Ngoc Kinh"* (Diamond Palace), or Nirvana (according to Buddhism). You see: All these classes are heavenly ones.
But there are similar hellish classes. The Daemon has thus imitated God to organize his own hierarchy with corresponding positions for the sole purpose of punishing

and harming you. I felt compelled to grant him this tremendous privilege of attempting to seduce and induce you to become his servants.

I have always said that there should be justice because that is God's law.** I have, at times, lost many of my disciples to him. I have already clearly shown you the different ways: the good and the evil.

I have also shown you the direction to follow to not become lost. You should be aware that demons have reincarnated throughout the 3,000 worlds and even among the 72 earths.

Unfortunately, these demons are innumerable and they are masters of illusion and seduction.

This is why I have said that I have placed many ferocious beasts among you and have ordered them to devour you; however, I have also given each of you an armor to protect yourself. This armor is your virtue and it is invisible to these beasts.

Thus, your virtue is the way to exterminate the demons and to return you to Me in Nirvana. If you do not follow the Great Way, you will become the demons' servants. I have said that your virtue is like an endless ladder which could help you to reach the highest position, My level. I may also lower Myself to elevate you.

I tell you again that even if one fulfills one's duty honestly and justly, s/he will still have to reincarnate after death again and again, if s/he does not cultivate the self spiritually by following the Great Way. So, when can s/he return to Me? Anyone can return to me after even after only one lifetime, if s/he will spend that life in self-cultivation. This is an enormous privilege I have given you in order to save all human beings. Alas, unfortunately, I have not often had the pleasure of seeing those who have accomplished this. Therefore, I repeat: You should admire and respect the Great Way.

Translator's note:

* The earth, where we are living, is the 68th among 72 earths.
**According to God's law, it would be unfair for humans to have no challenges in their way of self-cultivation to return to Nirvana. Thus, God has granted the Demon the privilege of attempting to seduce many away from the Great Way.

Thầy các con

Các con phần nhiều biết tiếng Langsa.
Thầy dùng nói cho các con hiểu Đạo-Lý.
Qu'est-ce que la noblesse, la richesse, la gloire?
La noblesse est l'ensemble de titres plus ou moins enivrants décernés aux hommes par les hommes.
Quelle est la valeur de ces titres?
N'est-ce pas suivant la valeur de ceux qui les donnent?
Donnés pas un humain, ils ne sont que trop humains. Ce qui vient d'un homme n'a rien de résistant. C'est sujet à détérioration. Ils sont détruits dès qu'on enlève la vie de celui qui les détient. Cherchez la Noblesse céleste, c'est la seule éternelle
La richesse est l'ensemble de toute préciosité qu'on ramasse en ce monde.
Que comprend-elle?
L'or, l'argent, la pourpre, la soierie etc...
L'or, l'argent ne sont que simples métaux.
La pourpre n'est que couleur.
La soierie n'est que matière animale.
Prenez-vous toutes ces choses en vraies richesses?
Elles ne sont qu'insignifiantes d'après leur provenance.
Cherchez, vous autres, la Richesse en la Vertu de Dieu, c'est la seule que vous aurez éternellement; nul ne pourra vous la dérober.
La gloire est souvent contre la vertu. Elle est éphémère. Elle provient souvent de la fourberie. La Gloire de Dieu est la seule qui résiste à toutes épreuves.
(Trung bạch: Mấy con phải làm sao mà tìm đặng la Noblesse, la Richesse et la Gloire de Dieu?)
Thầy trả lời: "Tu."

12-19-1926:

YOUR MASTER,

The majority of you, children know French. I will use French to make it easier for you to understand.

What is nobility, richness, and glory? The nobility is the gathering of titles which are given by men for more or less seducing men.

What is the value of those titles? Isn't it the value of those who gave them? Donned by human, they are just too human. What come from a human being are but not lasting. They are subject for deterioration: they are destroyed as soon as the life of the bearer is taken away. Go for celestial nobility, it is the only eternal. Richness is all the precious things that one gathers on this earth.

What does it contain? Gold, silver, velvet, silk, etc...

Gold and silver are but simple metals. Velvet is just a color. Silk is but material derived from animals. Do you see those as real preciosity? They are insignificant as their origin is appraised. Children, search for divine richness. That's the only you possess eternally; nobody can take it away from you.

Glory is in many instances against virtue. It is transient. It, many times, comes from dishonesty. Divine glory is the only which resists all challenges.

(Trung asked: How can we attain divine nobility, divine richness, and divine glory?) The Master replied: "TU" (self cultivation).

Dai Dan Cho Lon, December 20, 1926

YOUR MASTER, children.

Listen, disciples!
The Tao needs to have tenets in order to approach perfection, and for you to follow to avoid error. Some of you, thanks to their meritorious service, were employed in an important task so that they would be happy and have opportunities to progress. Unexpectedly, they did not respect My orders, have created criticism and quarrels. Do they deserve to be disciplined?
If I don't have the mercy to guide them forthwith, they will be disciplined more severely by Saints and Angels! You should regulate yourselves in your religious practice.
Listen, attendants! The Tao is guiding humanity; the holy way pilots earthly people. You are lucky to be born at the time when the Tao is founded, but if you do not cultivate your self to reach Nirvana, you would face regret later, all in vain for being downfallen.
Because of love of humanity, I have opened the Third Universal Salvation to save blessed people. Time is running out. Make haste, for Immortals and Buddhas at the triune-faith convention will propose closing the gates of the Tao. At that time, even though I desire to redeem you, I could not act against the divine mechanism.

December 24, 1926

JADE EMPEROR, or CAO DAI TIEN ONG DAI BO TAT MA HA TAT, TEACHING THE GREAT WAY FOR THE SOUTHERN QUARTER

Greetings to all children.

Children, if I said I have endured many hardships since the beginning of the faith in order to spread the Tao this rapidly, I should be very happy for you....Why am I sad? Children, you have suffered too much on this earth.... For ten thousand years, you were separate, under the power of evil. From My throne, *Huynh Kim Khuyet* at the White Pearl Palace, I have come to redeem you. Theoretically, I should decrease your sufferings, but instead, I have established the New Codes to discipline you; that's why I am sad! In reality, the New Codes that I ask you together to establish would bear upon your virtues as Immortals and Buddhas; that's why I have to accept fate; The White Pearl Palace would not accept anyone who is against these Codes.

You have to try your best to accomplish your duty in the establishment of the New Codes. Thai Bach will come to monitor your endeavors.

Dai Dan Cho Lon, December 27, 1926

YOUR MASTER, children.

Listen all disciples!
Many of you don't have sincerity in worshipping Me. In setting an altar in the house, some just wish to have some personal profit to their family, but not to seek a source of purity, to wash away their earthly offenses. Many of them are even more confused: they understand neither the meaning of setting up the altar, nor even the reason for the founding of the Tao.
Alas! In stepping into the path of the Tao, they did not dedicate time to search and study the Tao; do they then expect as disciples to be useful at all for the sacred faith? The Tao was opened just three times, but people have been sinful millions of times. Being born unto the earth, and having left their missions unrealized, they have passed away, returned to the initiatory center to report their earthly accomplishment. But they have not been able to accomplish anything, neither for their physical body nor for their spiritual duty, so how could they be useful for the Tao and for the human condition? Your conscience is a sacred gift from Me which is used to amend for your mistakes and to reward your humanitarian services. Doing right is from the Divine will; committing misdeeds is against the celestial laws. Any right or wrong acts are recorded by Angels and Saints for the final judgment. Try to understand.

Cau Kho, January 8, 1927

YOUR MASTER, children!

I am gratified that human beings have the compunction to surmount the long and difficult road to come walk together on the spiritual path.

You have only to realize that as human beings, you have to follow the Tao; if you do not, you cannot be fully human-a human recognizes right from wrong. If you are still confused, how can you reach your goal quickly?

You have to unite and cooperate with each other, put aside all secular misconceptions in order to be enlightened. I encourage you to use all your talents. Don't be shy and waste the sacred light that I have granted to you.

Try to understand!

Cho lon, January 10, 1927.

JADE EMPEROR, or CAO DAI TIEN ONG DAI BO TAT MA HA TAT, TEACHING THE GREAT WAY FOR THE SOUTHERN QUARTER

Listen, disciples.

Just as birds come back to their origin and water goes away, so too are people on this earth merely travelers. In order to accomplish their mission, they must be able to endure and abide suffering. Endurance will lead them back to their origin (1), and sufferance will expose them to different bad and good experiences of life.

Life consists of a mixture of glory and richness, which are but a dream. Every person must accomplish their mission assigned by God, whatever that may be, so that when they leave this earth, they may report the result to God. Whoever has fulfilled their mission will earn a higher position (2). Whoever has failed, and has committed crimes toward humanity, will be sent to a much darker and colder dimension where they will repent so that they may return to the right way to their origin. Otherwise, they will stay there to learn the way, life after life. Even the Genies and the Saints cannot escape reincarnation if they do not follow the way of self cultivation.

The Southern Quarter is well blessed by receiving God's light which guides people to escape from darkness and ignorance. Cultivating their virtues, staying contented, using simple attire, not forsaking wealth--all these are considered means to enlightenment. Detachment from things of this world is difficult. The way to heaven is small and the road is narrow: only a few ever find it. However, the way to hell is broad and its gate is wide enough for all people who choose its easy way (3).

The Great Way has come to earth to guide people; without it even Holy Water would not be able to wash away all sufferance.

Translator's notes:
(1) All living beings are part of God's spirit. Sooner or later, with self cultivation, they will come back to their origin, which is God.
(2) Higher position on their way back to their origin.
(3) Matthew 7: 13-14

Tayninh, January 16, 1927
The 13th day of the 12th month of the year of the Yang Fire Tiger

THAI BACH

Congratulations to all disciples. Great joy! Great joy!
Thuong Tuong Thanh, observe and do as I do.
Confucianist Chuong Phap (Censor Cardinal), it's your turn.
Tho, sit down. Stand up in two rows. Chuong Phap, Dau Su sit down. The three Phoi Su step forward. Thai Tho Thanh has to bring the New Codes that you have all compiled to the three Dau Su. These latter, all at the same time, stand up, and respectfully receive the New Codes so that their six hands lay on the book of New Codes. They then will offer the New Codes book to the Chuong Phap. The Chuong Phap, in turn, shall respectfully receive the book, hold it over their heads and walk to the altar and put the book there upon it. Listen, I now assign the two Chuong Phap to revise the book of New Codes, finishing within one month, then submit to the Ho Phap, who will evoke me to edit. Use a quiet room as the Hiep Thien Dai (Heavenly Union Palace). All the 12 zodiacal dignitaries have to be present; so should be the Thuong Sanh and Thuong Pham.
You have to evoke me again for further direction. The two Chuong Phap have to leave the book of the New Codes at the foot of my image overnight.
Duong has to wear the headdress like Luat.
Nuong has to wear the costume like Tho's.
After leaving the book of the New Codes on the altar, you may return to your seats.
All celestial appointees prostrate in front of the Master.

Re-evocation.

THAI BACH

The miraculous celestial laws are still missing in the New Codes that you have compiled.
(Laughter.)
I don't blame you: how could you know?
What a mishap! Without this secret, miraculous mechanism, there would not be laws and there would not, subsequently, be the Tao. (Laughter.)
I will pray to our eminently gentle, greatly merciful Master to allow adding these important secret elements to the New Codes. You have to pray with me. You have to ask all disciples of all temples to pray together with me with all sincerity from your hearts.
As the Tao is so important, you are important to guide and raise the state of human beings. From now on, I will take care of you more diligently. If I must discipline you, it's just because I want to increase your value. Please do not mind and be disturbed by it.

January 17, 1927
The 4th day of the 12th month of the year of the Yang Fire Tiger

Children, YOUR MASTER.

Thuong Trung Nhut, being the elder brother, you have to teach your younger brothers. As I have said, I founded the genuine Tao for you. Anything which is false is not from Me. I have come to teach humanity peace without conflict. I have also said, true honor is not on this earth. I have founded for your country the genuine faith to save all living beings. Thanks to the Tao, your country and you would attain great eminence. Whence do such positions of eminence arise? They are the result of your virtue. It is natural that the virtuous will ultimately overcome the cruel. As the Supreme Being, upholding ultimate justice, do you imagine that I do not have the power to do all things Myself but have need of your hands? You are chastened only for your lack of virtue. From this day forward, you have only to have faith in Me, to obey Me: thus reforming your virtue. Anything against the genuine Tao is from evil.
I bless you.

Tay Ninh, January 18, 1927.
The 15th of the 12th month of the year of the Yang Fire Tiger.

JADE EMPEROR, or CAO DAI TIEN ONG DAI BO TAT MA HA TAT, TEACHING THE GREAT WAY FOR THE SOUTHERN QUARTER

Children, all human beings! Celestial appointees, sit down! Children, listen!
Why to abstain from alcohol?
I have taught that your body is composed of a mass of everlasting spirits. You should understand that the internal organs of your body are also formed by living units whose function, whether they are aware of or not, is commanded by Me. I therefore use your body to teach.
Firstly, let's explain why alcohol is harmful to your physical body. Your physical body is still like animal and needs to eat in order to live. When alcohol is ingested, it is absorbed into all internal organs of your body including the heart which is the main machine for life. It makes your heart work more than naturally, it pushes the whole cardio-vascular system to function excessively, and the lungs do not have enough time to purify dirty blood (to oxygenate blood) which will be accumulated in the whole body, intoxicate the living units leading to progressive sickness and finally to demise of the living units of the organs and then of your body. Many people had half of their body dead just because of alcohol.
Secondly, I explain why alcohol is harmful to your spirit. I said that the soul forms your second body. It is the *"Khi"* which surrounds your body like a mold. Its center is the brain, the gate by where your second body enters or gets out is the fontanelle on top of the head which is watched and protected by the *Ho Phap*. With meditation, there is unification of The *"Tinh"* and the *"Khi"* and the *"Than"* leading to enlightenment.

The brain is thus the origin of the *"Khi."* When dirty blood is accumulated in the brain, it becomes confused and your spirit is not clear and calm to control the body. The body will lose its human personality and act like animals, and will have no hope to progress to the state of Genie, Saint, Immortal, and Buddha. At the same time, when the brain is confused, it becomes an open gate, the evil will take advantage to invade you and push you into crimes and subsequently into continuous reincarnation.

Therefore, listen, I forbid you to drink alcohol!

I ascend.

January 18, 1927
The 15th day of the 11th month of the year of the Yang Fire Tiger

JADE EMPEROR, or CAO DAI TIEN ONG DAI BO TAT MA HA TAT, TEACHING THE GREAT WAY FOR THE SOUTHERN QUARTER

Greetings to disciples, all male and female human beings! Calm down, calm down.
Living beings have not recognized how precious and honorable the Tao is. The Tao, as carried forth by human beings, united with the sacredness from Me, is to grow and expand across the universe. Whoever recognizes the Tao is blessed; whoever does not is unfortunate. Understand! I grant your application to the faith. I mercifully accept all of you tonight and allow the local angel of the village to teach you, as is his responsibility.
I ascend.

Than Hoang Bon Canh (Local Angel of the village)

Greetings to all celestial appointees. Greetings to disciples and all people, male and female, of the village.
I, the angel of the village, have the reputation of helping people from the four corners of the world,
Having received the blessing and appointment from our Master.
I am helping citizens to live in peace and order,
With continuous prosperity.
I receive your sincere prayers with beneficence,
And you have my blessings again and again.
All citizens abide in peace and order, Living in safety and honoring the Tao.

Since the time when I received the order from our Master to govern this village, I have been caring for the people with all my heart and with all my might, so that they may have a peaceful and happy life with successful crops every year. Today I receive the order from our Master to come to teach you about the Tao. You could not realize the miraculous celestial arrangement made many thousands of years ago. Listen, the last era is about to end; 90 percent of humanity will be destroyed. Alas! What a sadness! But no one can change the divine mechanism. The only thing that you can do is to be stricken of conscience, to cultivate self, to open your heart for humanitarian services, and come together to pray to God for the fate of humanity. The Supreme Being, Jade Emperor and all Buddhas, Immortals, and Saints, have founded the Third Universal Salvation to save humanity, awash as humanity is in an ocean of suffering. If you meet the Bat Nha Boat (Boat to Nirvana) and do not take the opportunity to embark, you will not be saved. Dignitaries presiding ceremonies!

Come kneel in front of the altar for me to bless you.

What a joy! What a happiness! Almost all citizens have recognized the Tao. From now on, I will pay all my heart and my attention to taking care of the village. I will let you know why. Since I received the order of our Master to help disciple Cao, I became more worried. Any time when there are accidents or epidemics of infectious diseases, I come to teach you how to avoid damage.

Regarding the offerings, I prefer you to use vegetarian foods and fruits in order to avoid killing.

I will explain about ceremony:

Ceremony is from your faith. The offerings are to show your respect. Saints and Angels will never be able to use these offerings. Therefore it's better for you to use fruits. The offerings are from your heart. I will not condemn you; it's just the tradition. I want you to follow the Supreme Being's holy will. What do you think? Try to respond! (Laughter.)

Good-bye! I depart.

Session at An Hoa, January 22, 1927
(The 19th day of the 12th month of the year of the Yang Fire Tiger)

JADE EMPEROR, or CAO DAI,
TEACHING THE GREAT WAY FOR THE
SOUTHERN QUARTER

Greetings to disciples and all human beings.
This is the first encounter of your country with Myself, so many suspicions still remain.
By way of overwhelming compassion, you and I will spread the path without fearing difficulty or worrying about dishonest persons. You shall march ahead; they will recognize later what is right and what is wrong. I am pleased with you and admit you all, male and female.
Tuong, you have to teach them the necessary knowledge. I give here a general poem:
There is but one sky for this universe of impermanence,
The people, only grains of sand upon the firmament.
When caressed by still water, they are content and composed;
Caught by storm and wave, their peace is dashed against stones.
Having been spun on the karmic wheel without cessation,
For the want of an instant of self-cultivation, they have known to be able to escape from reincarnation.
Yet behold from the South land gusts a fair wind,
The reign of the redeeming Tao about to begin.
Allow all the females in to hear My teachings!
Dear beloved female disciples, I bring the Third Salvation, with no discrimination between stature tall or small, or state of richer or poorer. I only wish that you do virtuous deeds every day, following the humanistic teachings; for example, keeping the four virtues (*Cong, Dung, Ngon, Hanh:* good

work, good appearance, good speech, and good personality, respectively).

The morality of the country of the South is always good; it is just that those among you who are corrupted, I have to remind you of the good way!

Now the males, come in! Listen carefully!

Do you know why you see injustice every day?

Do you know why officers abuse their power over the people, children disobey their parents, and people are not faithful to their friends, creating disturbances in moral principles? Because of lack of spirituality!

I bless you all, children. I ascend.

January 26, 1927
The 23rd day of the 12th month of the year of the Yang Fire Tiger

JADE EMPEROR, or CAO DAI, TEACHING THE GREAT WAY FOR THE SOUTHERN QUARTER

Greetings to disciples, and all human beings.
Listen:

The ship upon the celestial sea awaits a fair wind,
To bear the people of the South aloft from Earth toward Heaven.
In donning brown vestments, you strive for Nirvana,
In cultivating conscience, you disdain wealth and honor.
The clockwork of the heavens tells its time true,
Striking the hour the Divine may rain down upon you.
Bear well the travails of conscience in this life;
You will soon be removed from this earthly realm of strife.
The Great Way has been founded three times, yet Earthly people still commit many grievous errors. They still become lost in the material world and disregard virtuous principles taught by saints and sages of old. This life full of hypocrisy is short, and yet they fight for wealth and pursue honor. Being born as a human being conveys upon you a special mission; yet people pay no heed to the essentials of the journey, from giving back to their parents, to paying back the debt they owe their country, instead immersing themselves in a life that only leads to worry and sadness, denying the holy virtues, using delusion to satisfy the senses.
Time will not wait for such as these. Life's journey is difficult and tiring, and Death will prove all wealth and honor to have been but a dream.
Your day of reckoning will soon be upon you at the *Nghiet Canh Dai* (storehouse of the Akashic records; a place where the dead review their actions in previous lives, the equivalent

to St. Peter's Gate). Life after life, you will continue to reimburse the Universe for the errors of your ways until you are enlightened. Such is the fate of mortals. The Tao exists to guide people along the path of righteousness and piety, and thereby dismount the Karmic wheel, escaping reincarnation and reaching Nirvana at last. Make haste unto the path to quicken your reward and avoid continuous suffering. The Tao is an open secret; don't lose sight of the fact, continual self-examination is required for its perpetual discovery.
Try to comprehend, human beings!

Cho Lon, January 31, 1927

YOUR MASTER, children.

Time has flown, and it is spring once again. The landscape has not changed, but the people's hearts have been transformed. The Tao has progressed quickly; compared with last year, the Tao's wisdom is now shining ever more brightly in human life. I am delighted to see your heartfelt efforts to magnify the Tao, to bring people closer to each other. You have traveled the thorny path to people's hearts. Some local disciples do not yet carry the Tao because of their secular obligations. Ly Thai Bach is therefore planning to organize a great ceremony at Cau Kho temple so that all the disciples can more easily come together in a display of unity.

T., you will have to join in to preside over the ceremony for your younger brothers. You disciples here should do the same.

Cau Kho Temple, February 1st, 1927

I am disappointed for the ones who are absent today. Time has passed quickly and you are still hesitant. The Path is so monumentally great and profound that your earthly minds cannot fathom. If you do not transcend your secular attachments, your travails in following Me for the last year would have been wasted. The earthly life has so much torment to begin with, and you live in a most difficult time, so you should contemplate spirituality more; otherwise, you condemn yourself to immersion in the material world forever, battling for wealth and power like the run of the mill.

You have to direct your energies toward spreading My way; thus you can both maintain your valuable traditions and still escape rebirth in the Earthly plane. I will not reveal the celestial mechanism behind it all, but you have only to understand that as a human, you are in the highest position among Earthly beings; you must cultivate an extraordinary mind to be worthy of being human. You should understand that I have created many races with their own special, sacred characteristics. Only because human beings do not try to discover the truth and because they instead obsess on outward profits, negating the profits of their conscience, killing and not loving, looking to harm but not looking to understand each other, do they suffer.

Once you comprehend the Universal justice in My way and come together under Universal love, you would satisfy God's will and be abundantly blessed. Understand!

Tay Ninh, February 1st, 1927
The 1st day of the 1st month of the year Dinh Mao

Taoist Chuong Phap Tuong.

Greetings to all disciple brothers and sisters.
Joy…Joy…Joy….Happiness…Happiness…Happiness…
Great blessings to humanity and to this 68th earth. I should have more merits in order to be admitted to the 36 heavens. All thanks to the guidance of our great and gentle Father. I am telling you, brothers and sisters, value your precious celestial position. Don't be reticent on the path. Remember my name when fighting against evil seductions.
For myself, even though I didn't have enough accumulated merit, technically, I still attain this position. If you guide and save the whole of humanity, your position would be much, much higher!
Think about it, and be happy in your practicing of the Tao.

JADE EMPEROR, or CAO DAI, TEACHING THE GREAT WAY FOR THE SOUTHERN QUARTER

Children, greetings to you,
Trung, Cu, Tac, do you remember how it was this time last year? And you see how it is now?
Beloved daughters Trinh and Hieu, have you seen how I have kept My promise? This time last year when I founded the Great Way, I had but twelve disciples. Four of them fell wayward and succumbed, so then I had only eight left; but two of those were so indolent, they did not practice the Tao. Even a great Buddha, who incarnates to this earth, without Me, would not be able to guide more than forty thousand human beings at once in so short a time.

I am happy, and congratulate all My forty thousand disciples. Tho, you are very dedicated, and your dedication has redeemed many people. I congratulate you.

Binh, I promote you to the *Phoi Su* as a reward for your love and your virtue. Thanks to you, humanity will be able to escape the ocean of suffering.

Ban, I promote you to the *Giao Su* and Tro the *Giao Huu*. And many others, too. Call them back here on the 9th of the month for Thai Bach to reward them. I bless you all, even if you are not here.

I lift the handle of the *Ngoc Co* (Basket with beak) for you to pass beneath for Me to bless. I wish you all to be dedicated like Tho, and self-cultivate like saints, for the Great Way shall be known all over the world, and disciples will increase exponentially, and your responsibilities will grow heavier and heavier.

If you love Me, you would love the Tao, and subsequently love human beings. If you value Me, you would value the Tao and subsequently value living beings.

In this coming first month of the year, Thai Bach will gather the female disciples in order to establish the female college. I rely on you.

I bless you.

I ascend.

THAI BACH

The Sacerdotal Council. Listen.

I grant ceremonial costume to the female college. Comply, and from now on, use these beautiful costumes for ceremonies, according to the hierarchy.

All female dignitaries are to work under the female *Dau Su* (Cardinal) who in turn has to obey the *Giao Tong* (Pope) and the *Chuong Phap* (Censor Cardinal).Female *Dau Su* are also elected according to the New Codes established by the Sacerdotal Council. They are to obey the orders of the Sacerdotal Council both spiritually and temporally.Female *Dau Su* wear a costume similar to the one for the male *Dau Su*. The white silk robe has nine ribbons and is embroidered with lotus flowers. The head covering is a hood like the one worn by nuns and is also made of white silk. The hood is overlaid with a golden headdress called *Phuong Thien Mao,* and the top of it is embossed with the Divine Eye surrounded by a golden circle. She wears white *Vo Uu* shoes (worriless shoes) with the calligraphic character *"Huong"* (Fragrance) on the toes. Comply with these instructions! Female *Phoi Su* (Archbishops) are to wear a similar costume without *Phuong Thien Mao*. Their robes have three ribbons. On the chest is embroidered the Divine Eye surrounded by a golden circle. Comply with these instructions!

Female *Giao Su* (Bishops) are to wear a robe with three ribbons, with the white silk hood, but without shoes.

Female *Giao Huu* (Priestesses) wear costumes like the *Giao Su's,* but without headdress, and instead, a white lotus with the Divine Eye in the center is pinned into their hair.

Female *Le Sanh* (Student Priestesses) wear a costume like the *Giao Huu.* They cover their head with a long veil knotted at the nape so that the two ends of unequal lengths hang down. A white lotus flower is pinned into their chignon.

Our Master observes the absence of many sisters and will not grant any appointment. Sister Lam Huong Thanh! You are to invite all female disciples to come the 15th day of this month for appointment by our Master and for the establishment of the female college.

Tay Ninh, February 5th, 1927
The 4th day of the 1st month of the year Dinh Mao

THAI BACH.

Greeting to all disciples, brothers and sisters, and all living beings. Good gathering!
Such sorrow for humanity! Such misery for humanity!
Human beings are too cruel. Their crimes deserve just punishment. But because of love for humanity, I have tried in vain to pray for the amnesty of human beings during the ten-day convention at the *Bach Ngoc Kinh* (the White Pearl Palace). Yet, I could not act against Divine Justice. Human destruction shall afflict you through your mutual killing, and deadly diseases. I have been heartbroken, prostrated and praying at the *Bach Ngoc Kinh,* but finally had to accept the fate of humanity. I am even sadder in seeing human beings in confusion and ignorance. Needless to say, even in this small country, Vietnam, with its sacred ground here, I could not procure amnesty for cities such as Saigon, Cho Lon, Gia Dinh, Hue, Hai Phong and Hanoi. What a tragedy! What a tragedy! What a tragedy!

Notes of the translator: We are all much too familiar with the succeeding tragedies in Vietnam, occurring since 1945 in the struggles for power from North to South and resulting in the deaths of thousands upon thousands of people, both from Vietnam and intervening powers.

24-12-26
JADE EMPEROR, or CAO DAI, TEACHING THE GREAT WAY FOR THE SOUTHERN QUARTER

I, your Master, am happy to see you all gathering here tonight to show your sincere respect. I congratulate you disciples, sons and beloved daughters, for your virtues. Your gathering here is not only for the faith but also because of your mutual love. This day last year you were still confused in your earthly dreams; the path had somewhat lessened your secular attachments but not enough for you to be totally dedicated to the Tao. And the time has rushed by, with enormous changes in people's hearts, including a relinquishment of wisdom in lieu of honor and riches, and abuse of the Tao for personal gain. I am still holding open the secret, Divine mechanism, hoping that you will try with all of your might to institute the Tao in order to redeem people, to help them surmount their weaknesses, and together walk the elusive path to Nirvana, that even many sages of old have missed.

I have to mention that many of you have not put all your heart into serving the Tao. Realize that, through mercy, I have appointed you to certain celestial positions in order for you to redeem your karma. However, many of you with heavy secular obligations still have not recognized the hardship of self-cultivation as a ladder to help to escape from reincarnation. You must realize that, lacking My mercy, your mistakes would be recorded and you would not have further opportunity to serve humanity and thereby redeem yourselves.

Before praying to Me in the evening, you should ask yourself in your best conscience if you have completed your duties of the day, or have done anything against your conscience. If your duties were left incomplete, or your conscience was left unsatisfied, you must repent. This will serve to make you more and more holy day by day. My hope for each of you is that you would tend heartily to your self-improvement, so then both the Tao would benefit from your efforts, and you would set a good example for others. You are to love one another; your guidance to and sharing with each other are precious gifts which please Me greatly.

February 1927

Quan Am Boddhisattva of the South Sea

Greetings to disciples, brothers and sisters, all living beings. Celestial appointees sit down. Listen, sisters.

I am so delighted to see you sisters practicing the Tao. You must also get together to guide younger sisters. Many sisters who have not given their all for the Tao must endeavor to be more worthy of the love of the Supreme Being. I am happy with those sisters who have endured hardship to complete their duties. That's what I expect from you all.

THAI BACH

All friends, be in order and solemnity to greet the Supreme Being.

JADE EMPEROR, or CAO DAI, TEACHING THE GREAT WAY FOR THE SOUTHERN QUARTER

Children, listen. Wherever I abide is the holy land. I have ordained to promote the local angel to the Van Xuong position to govern Hiep Ninh village, to teach the Tao to people, and to have the ultimate power of reward and punishment over the local people until they should repent. So, people of Long Thanh village, don't worry.

Regarding the Holy See, I want to see unity between God's will and man's power. That's My virtue that you should watch and imitate.

Since the time I founded the Tao for you, I have never done anything by Myself alone. Wherever you choose that pleases the Sacerdotal Council would please Me. You have to get together to attend to the matter of the Holy See. Everything should be at Tay Ninh. You have understood My Holy will about spending; be economic, spend only what is necessary.

February 13th, 1927 (the 12th day of the first month of the year Dinh Mao)

JADE EMPEROR, or CAO DAI, TEACHING THE GREAT WAY FOR THE SOUTHERN QUARTER

Children, all disciples, heed me!
The *Hiep Thien Dai* is the sacred place where I reign to preserve the sacred power of the faith. As long as the Tao endures, the *Hiep Thien Dai* still exists. Moreover, the *Hiep Thien Dai* is the place where the *Giao Tong* comes and communicates with the 36 Heavens, the 3000 Worlds, the 68 planets and the 10 courts of Hell to beg the salvation of humanity.
As I have warned, the five branches of the Great Way are rendered profane by the incarnate believers who day by day move further from fidelity with the Tao, completely degrading the significance of the holy doctrine. For this reason I have resolved to come to teach My children Myself, not to entrust the teaching of My holy doctrine any longer to imperfect incarnate beings.
I have already spoken about spiritual power; I shall now speak to you about temporal powers.
The *Hiep Thien Dai* is placed under the authority of the *Ho Phap* (Legislative Protector). He is assisted by the *Thuong Sanh* (Director in Secular Affairs) and by the *Thuong Pham* (Director in Spiritual Affairs). I have chosen the 12 Zodiacal dignitaries in increments of three:

    1- Under the *Ho Phap,* who is concerned with Law and Justice:
    Hau is *Bao Phap* (1) (Juridical Conservator)
    Duc is *Hien Phap* (Juridical Renovator)
    Nghia is *Khai Phap* (Juridical Reformer)
    Trang is *Tiep Phap* (Juridical Legislator)

This branch is concerned with the conservation and application of the religious laws, temporally and spiritually. Every transgression of the laws is brought to the awareness of the *Hiep Thien Dai*.

Under The *Thuong Pham*, who is concerned with spiritual affairs:

Chuong is *Bao Dao* (Religious Conservator)
Tuoi is *Hien Dao* (Religious Renovator)
Dai is *Khai Dao* (Religious Reformer)
Trong is *Tiep Dao* (Religious Legislator) (2)

This branch is concerned with the meditation cells and temples. He supervises all disciples and defends them against the abuses of authorities.

Under the *Thuong Sanh*, who is concerned with temporal affairs:

Phuoc is *Bao The* (Temporal Conservator)
Manh is *Hien The* (Temporal Renovator)
Thau is *Khai The* (Temporal Reformator)
Vinh is *Tiep The* (Temporal Legislator)

I exhort you to maintain personal impartiality in your functions. Do not forget that anyone who has great power has a heavy burden of responsibility.

I bless you.

(1) Bao is to conserve
Hien is to offer
Khai is to initiate
Tiep is to accept

(2) Mr. Cao Duc Trong is the last appointee among the 12 Zodiacal dignitaries.

Cau Kho, February 19, 1927

February 19th, 1927

YOUR MASTER, children.

In accordance with Justice and the request from the Triune-Faith Court, I appointed you as dignitaries. In reality, not many of you appointees are worthy for the term. Therefore, once appointed, you should remain humble and remember your responsibility; and whoever has not been appointed should not be sad and abandon your virtue. Understand!
I would be pleased if you would try to build up your merit yourselves. It would be useless for you to be accepted into the Tao, appointed to a celestial position, yet be without redeeming qualities or virtues.
Understand!

Opening Ceremony at Phuoc Long Temple.
Cho Dem, March 1, 1927

YOUR MASTER, children.

The spiritual transformation of human beings is in accordance with the transformation of Heavens and Earth. Everyone who has affinity with Creation likes to find quietness among Nature for meditation. Many others, although capable of the same affinities, are not true to them; they do not gear their activities toward noble acts but instead toward cruelty and crime: they act against the Divine will, and disregard reincarnation and karma. They think of life as the fleeting moment; they conspire for wealth, power and gluttony.

I would challenge you: where does the noble part of the human mind go after the body's death, the part embracing within it Love, Hatred, Joy, Remorse? Do you think such a mind simply disintegrates?

Each of you should meditate on this question and pursue an answer. If you find an appropriate answer, you are a person who realizes the Tao; otherwise, you are of feeble mind.

I ask you women to follow the three womanly duties and the four virtues; and you males to follow the three male duties and the five virtues of Confucianism. If you fulfill your human duties, you would be well received by the Tao. Heed My words!

Dai Dan Cau Kho, March 5, 1927

JADE EMPEROR, or CAO DAI, TEACHING THE GREAT WAY FOR THE SOUTHERN QUARTER

Many of you may think that being CaoDai disciples, one has to be totally detached from secular activities, dreaming day and night that you might only find a secluded place for meditation. I would let you know that if you have not paid all your karmic debt, and have not accrued enough merit, you cannot become enlightened. In order to be enlightened, you must first accrue enough merit by spreading the Tao and guiding human beings. If such is against your nature, you may then find other ways by which to attain the coveted position of enlightenment. You have to understand My holy will in order to cultivate your mind and set up your goals. Any path you choose to walk, you have to have a sacred guiding light; you have to have a goal in order to succeed, whether you want to be a king, a teacher, a technician, or a Taoist. Any profession would be sufficient except that in which you do not act as a professional.

Dear, beloved women! You keep looking up to nobility and the wealthy, and complain that you are not enough blessed, while you look down your nose and despise the lowly and poorer people. This is the height of immorality! I advice you to open your hearts and love people; that would please Me. You have to cultivate your virtue. Be modest to the superior and generous to the inferior. Obey this, children!

Male disciples, new disciples, listen, children.

Under the justice of the divine law, you have had to suffer. It's because you do not know how to cultivate the noble mind that I have bequeathed to you. Your mind is yet so narrow so that you do not progress and the path becomes increasingly difficult. Henceforth from your initiation, you must take heed to adhere to the right path, to guide each other clear of the thorny maze. Do not lose your character due to desire of personal profit: this would only squander the priceless sacred light that I have bestowed upon you. Heed Me!

April 5, 1927
YOUR MASTER, children.

Trung, because you have so many important responsibilities, I have asked T. to spread the Tao in the other provinces for you. You have safely negotiated a difficult turn in your path, thanks to which your future merits would be fulfilled. I have granted you and other disciples enough authority and responsibilities to perfect the Tao that I have begotten. You have to nurture it in order to become worthy; you must show patience in all things, surmounting difficulties to reach your goal. I have mercifully guided you with each step, and now it's your turn to use your enlightened mind to guide humanity. Young and old, you have to love and guide each other using your virtue as an example for the next generation. The path is still long and difficult, and once you will not have close communication with Me in the future, if you do not help and support each other, what then would you become?

I also need you to know that many *Giao Huu* (Priests) do not know their duties, so you have to teach them. They should know at least the origin of the Tao, and should learn My teachings and then take turns in teaching male and female disciples. Many of the *Giao Huu* know nothing about the Tao, and disciples cannot learn anything from them, so they are not useful for anything. You have to remind them to meet once a month with the Sacerdotal Council in order to learn how to teach. Obey!

I bless you all.

April 12, 1927.

YOUR MASTER, children.

Children, I have clearly felt those concerns about the Tao which are near to your hearts. Many of you wish the Genies and the Saints would punish the evil ones so that the Tao would be more stable and succeed faster. However, the divine mechanism takes no heed your earthly desires which are simply due to your human impatience. You should try not to hate but to have compassion for those unenlightened ones. With love and mercy in guiding you, I have designed the secret mechanism so that you may use your acquired holiness of mind to deal with even heretics, until the time when you have overcome your own karma. The Tao is steadfast. Be neither taken to excess, nor hesitant. Be patient and cooperative in clearing the thorny path for the generations to follow. The celestial guidebook has clearly spelled out many paths of action. Through love, I have taken care of the difficulties for you; you have only to complete your duty. Whoever puts all their efforts into the Tao will come back to be unified with Me. But whoever intends to disturb the Tao will be punished. The Triune-Faith Court has often times proposed to close the gate of the Tao, but I hadn't the heart to do it, due to your sincere efforts. Ly Bach / Li Po and Quan Am/ Quan Yin had recommended punishment of the evil ones, but I would not agree because I want you to experience a little more sufferance among them. ....If you have thought of Me, each of you will take haste to advance the Tao. In the old times, the Saints spent a lot of time arduously initiating the Tao.

Now, the Tao that was founded only a short age ago has become a glorious beacon which would be enough to pleasantly light your steps upon your journey

April 15, 1927 (Phu Nhuan)

YOUR MASTER, children.

You misunderstand the celestial mechanism in thinking that I am unable to subdue evil, and suffer the evildoers. You just wish to see them be punished, but that is not My Holy plan. If you yourself choose not to walk, I would not carry you through your life. Doing for yourself is therefore your concern. The Tao is founded in Justice and is already therefore a great blessing. If instead I carried you through this temporal world, you would not be wont to labor for the Tao. As long as you are witness to disappointment on this Earth, the Tao is not yet fulfilled.

You are the first to receive the Tao from Me; therefore, you should realize your great and noble responsibility. If you do not fulfill your duty you are not worthy. I advise you just to keep cultivating your heart, your virtue, to keep the Tao in order, all difficulty would be surmounted.

In practicing the Tao, you have to observe justice. Once justice is able to control violence, the Tao would be manifest. Understand!

April, 20, 1927

LY BACH

Friend Trung, I would like to let you know that many disciples of our Compassionate Master did not follow the teachings of our Master in order to fulfill their human duties in love and cooperative friendship, but instead create hatred among each other. I wish that you could set that issue straight. The Compassionate Master taught that there should be love, sharing, and cooperation in the promotion of the Tao. It has not been very long, and His teachings were not respectfully followed. What should happen in the future when there will be no more close communication from our Master? I want you to take time to straighten out this issue with the disciples. I will keep an eye on you.

Hatred and indifference among followers of the Tao would create animosity among people and only lead to chaos. They would relinquish the path, having been stained with this bloodshed and would be doomed to their loss of Heaven. Our Compassionate Master spoke that the Tao would be raised out of the determination of the disciples, especially of the celestially appointed dignitaries. For any issue related to the Tao, in order to please people's hearts you have to get together for discussion and have the consensus before implementation. That would make the Tao stable and strong. If there is any difficulty, it's your responsibility to guide all disciples to setting things straight. You have been granted the authority to make decisions, so if you get together for discussion and support, all would be well. Ever be mindful of your human duty, never to neglect it and become irreverent of the Holy will of our Compassionate Master. Take heed!

The 27th day of the fourth month of the year Dinh Mao (5-27-1927)

YOUR MASTER, children.

What's a such Sacerdotal Council? Children! How sad I am! What a tragedy! I thought I would not need to lecture upon it and had only to await your heightened spirituality in order for you to realize My concerns about humanity since the Creation of the race. But your mind has so been inundated by maya (the illusionary material world) that it has overlooked the holy spirit that I have granted to you. That's why I have to bring it up now.

Children! Do you know how much suffering I have endured each time I have labored to redeem you?

If you only knew the power of the Supreme Being, you would realize that it is a torturous trial for Me.

I have created human beings thinking that in establishing positions of Genies, Saints, Immortals, and Buddhas, I would show you that the holy spirit is higher than the earthly mind. However, the prize was only one out of a million, and this breaks My heart. Alone in you, since the creation of the whole universe, have I invested the best love of a gentle father; yet you children have despised your father and betrayed Me, akin to the Demon called Lucifer in Christianity. Genies, Saints, Immortals, and Buddhas have bemoaned your downfall.

In upholding justice, I must be impartial and apply the Divine law. But if I should enforce the letter of the law, you would be exiled to Hell forever. If you would put yourself in My position, the position of a father, you would know how much I have suffered for you.

Each time I suffered for you, I have incarnated to Earth to found the Tao to save you; in this I was maltreated by you, railed against and expelled by you, even killed by you. Alas! What a tragedy! What a tragedy! The Tao that I have labored to bequeath you is now in the hands of a Demon who has charmed and seduced your minds. If even the great spirits and Immortals were seduced, what could I expect from other spirits? I did not punish the Demon, so how could I punish you? But one cannot avoid the Divine law which I Myself must respect. You have committed your own crimes, and therefore will exact your own punishment, as even the Genies, Saints, Immortals, and Buddhas have done. I have blessed even My own enemy; how could I not bless you, My children? Except when you refuse My blessings. What a pity! What a hate! Each time I founded the Tao, I had to warrant My support for you exactly like a warranty against a loan. I am ultimately responsible for whatever crime that you commit. You have been given due time to cultivate yourselves yet you did not improve but committed more crimes instead. What an outrage! What would you have Me do; shall I desert the Tao to find other means of pursuing your redemption, so to be exiled along with you, or wait until the Tao eliminates Me?

Who would not suffer in slicing out one's own entrails? If I did not ask Thai Bach to postpone your punishment until the completion of the Holy See so that you may redeem yourselves through the personal merits wrought through service, there would not be one tenth of you left. You have to listen to My words in order to redeem yourselves. And you have to heed and respect Thai Bach's orders. I remind you one last time.

I bless you.

I ascend.

Session of May 29, 1927.

LY BACH

Greetings to disciples, male and female.
Be seated.

The Tao is erected through the virtuous minds and humble behavior of the disciples of the Compassionate Master. If one chooses to follow the Tao, yet still struggles and competes with the mind of an ordinary human, even though there be numerous disciples and a multitude of contributions, the Tao remains merely a phenomenon of the mortal plane. Due to human frailty, disciples themselves often generate obstacles which prevent the Tao from progressing, creating storm clouds over the firmament of the Tao. The Compassionate Master generously introduced a path of purity to the world to serve as the way to Heaven; but man, instead of purification, prefers to immerse himself instead in human failings, bringing calamity upon the heads of his brethren. Such behavior serves no one. But pay this no heed; I have my own way to correct that. Concentrate instead upon only fulfilling your own responsibility and do not bother yourselves with any others' wrongdoing. I assiduously follow our Father's will, without which there would be no possibility of redemption through meritorious service, and humanity would have no hope left though the wicked would neither be able to create chaos anymore. Black and white, two colors; good and bad, two ways; if one is strong and perseverant, it will succeed. Evil, evil; Buddha, Buddha--two different paths. Punishment and reward shall come accordingly.

June 1, 1927.

YOUR MASTER, children.

T..., from the establishment of the Tao for the spreading of the way until now, in general, disciples have been devoted to guiding humanity and building the Tao; those disciples whom I rely upon, clear away the thorns on the path to Heaven, guiding people out of the ocean of sufferings which is this world.

The Tao was established; the feet of many human disciples are well washed; however, children, you still meet with many difficulties in spreading the Way to the next generations. A bright horizon emerges above the wave, but the vessel of enlightenment depends upon the celestial mechanism, and can often be jolted aloft, with many lost to the abyss; those are the disciples who abandon the noble virtues and are wicked of deed and sully the reputation of the precious Tao that I have lovingly endowed to you. You have suffered for the Tao, enduring humiliation in the wearing of your brown costumes while serving as the example for future generations on their path to serenity. Dear disciples, keep following the right path through its twists and turns. The sum of your merits will assure the final state for each one of you. By the end of the 6th month, I will cease all recruiting séances. Use all your perseverance and sincerity to build the Tao henceforth. This is My last advice. Pay attention. Whoever is wicked molds their own fate. As for yourself, just keep following straight and narrow the path up the sacred spiritual ladder, awaiting the day of reunification with Me. That is the treasured way.

My blessings to you.

July 1927, Minh Ly Dan.

JADE EMPEROR, or CAO DAI, TEACHING THE GREAT WAY FOR THE SOUTHERN QUARTER

I greet you, children. Gather round. Greetings to all of you! (Laugh....) I am happy for you, Trung. I have assembled the Immortals and Buddhas to discuss establishing the Tao in the South. Children, follow My advice, do not argue among yourselves. Reach a consensus in solidarity in order to restore morality. Though there are many different branches, in the future there will be unity. Children, although you belong to different branches, love each other as brothers and sisters in the same family. Do not be jealous of each other and despise each other. I have set up this session because I knew you would be here. Trung, help Minh Ly. The Tao is like a house; it needs its principal column, secondary column, this beam and that. The smallest beam is as necessary as the largest. And though there are many, many beams to hold up this House, there is only one roof; only one Master reigns. Trung, train your disciples to know the laws and tenets of the Faith. The Tao is based on precepts. In Minh Ly, the seminary will train faithful disciples to redeem the souls of their fellow men. I will depart. Later, Thai At will come.
I ascend.

BOOK II

Tây Ninh (Gò Kén temple) Year of Yang Fire Tiger 1926.

YOUR MASTER, children!

What is the world?
How are human beings like guests in this world?
Why are they called guests?
The world is a place full of sufferings where Saints and Immortals who committed crimes are exiled to pay their Karmic debts. If they succeed, they may return to their original home (Nirvana) from whence they came, if not, they have to reincarnate again to the world. That's why their spirits are called guests.
What is the Tao?
Why is it called the Tao?
The Tao is a way that leads exiled Saints, Immortals, and Buddhas back to their original home. It is also a way for human beings to avoid reincarnation. Without the Tao, they would all be lost, and could not return to their initial positions. The Tao has deep meanings, one needs to know first the basic concepts in order to understand accurately and precisely further miraculous facts. The Tao and life are the same. Without the Tao, life would be meaningless. The Tao and life complement and help each other to be more enriched and meaningful. In following the Tao, one may cultivate self and lead a worry free and contented life, and nothing could be better.
That's miraculous and wise.
Ascension.

Tây Ninh (Gò Kén temple) Year of Yang Fire Tiger 1926.

Here is LY THAI BACH.

Regarding the election of the sub dignitaries, you erred against divine will, as one person could not hold so many responsibilities. Thượng Trung Nhựt, you are aware of that.

(Thượng Trung Nhựt addressed:....)

I concur with your change. You could not do that just because of lack of manpower. This is your own business. I would not interfere. You just need to follow one principle that one person could not hold two responsibilities. Thái Thơ Thanh could not be treasurer and deputy chief at the same time. (There should be two officers'signatures to issue money). It's against the administrative policy. Impartiality is very important in the great Tao. Obey!

I have some more recommendations: You should contribute your services to speed up the establishment of the administrative council, because many people are still floundering in the ocean of sufferings, and haven't had an opportunity to know the Tao. I have pity for them. What a misfortune for them. In the meanwhile, many others are fortunate enough to meet the Tao, but hesitate and want to go backward (because they have witnessed many troubles in the organization). I am worried for living beings. You should be the examples for people as religious persons. If the examples are good, the Tao would be bright. If not, what would happen to the Tao?

Many of you are occupied with secular life, and could not distinguish between right and wrong. In the congregation, when they confront with objections, they are dissuaded by non religious persons. What a shame for the virtuous person?

Dear brothers, if you listen to my words, please take care of the congregation and spread my words to all others. Many other disciples have also made great efforts. I will ask our Master for their promotion.

Good bye!

Ascension.

Saigon, Cao Thượng Phẩm's residence, the 12th day of the 6th month of the year Bính Dần (July 21, 1926)

JADE EMPEROR, or CAODAI, TEACHING THE TAO IN THE SOUTHERN QUARTER

All guests, all female disciples, listen.

If all the world practiced their faiths, the world could change the divine will and eliminate all disasters. If each individual practiced their own faith, the divine record would be shattered. What is practice of faith? It is the self-cultivation toward gentleness and kindness according to the divine plan. If all the people of the world are cruel, how could one maintain life? If one commits crimes against God, one would be punished. In this life, if one does not improve self, one would easily commit crimes against God. Divine positions are reserved for gentle and good people, but not for greedy ones. Although there are divine laws, the rewards would be judged by divine justice, not randomly and easily attained by just anyone. If it were easy to reach divine positions, everyone would be able to reach them with a little education, and then to avoid re-incarnation.

Scriptures help people to improve themselves and become enlightened; they can be compared to chopsticks that are necessary to serve meals, if there are no chopsticks, one may still use one's own hands to serve meals. Read again the scriptures, and try to contemplate on the divine justice to find the truth. You are better off to directly follow Me than go around seeking out scriptures.

Ascension.

The 27th day of the 6th month of the year Bính Dần (8-4-1926)

JADE EMPEROR

Greetings to all disciples,

I like you to gather together to listen to My teachings:

Th…, listen:

This is the era of destruction, all visible matters will be destroyed, therefore, The Third Universal Salvation was founded.

I come to move the Tao, re-establish the Nothingness. To you, which of the following is right? Visible matters or the Nothingness? Visible matters may be destroyed, but the Nothingness couldn't be.

Th…, I like you to visit to see with your own eyes Angkor Thom and Angkor Wat, which were recognized as extremely great. Are they perpetual? I recognize well your virtues, the era of falsehood has passed, and this is the time of sincerity. I don't want you to waste your wealth for falsehood. You don't need to build any holy temple, or to worship at the statue of The Buddha. You know that life's salvation is "My Original Holy Essence."

I recommend that you should just take care of human beings with all your heart. I will take care of their spirits. You don't know where the truth is, so you don't have to be worried about it. Your responsibility is great, so is your holy name. You should always obey My orders. You must establish an organization, co-operate with other disciples, progressively according to your capability, to build a school, a convalescence home for the elders, a children's center, and a meditation hall.

Don't worry about temples. In the future, I am afraid that you would not be able to administer all of them. Listen and obey. You have to follow Tr… to serve and save human beings. If you can provide ways for other children to go spreading the Tao, you should get together with them to arrange it.

Try to obey. Ascension.

HERE IS THE EIGHT FEMALE FAIRY.

Greetings to you, brothers and sisters. Please be seated.

In the New Year, at the new temple, with everything else also being new, I wish all brothers and sisters all new fortune, with all spiritual accoutrements for the practice of the Tao. I want to let you know, every year, during Springtime, whoever takes care of serving angels, Saints, Immortals, and Buddhas, would have double blessings as compared to regular times. As for the works assigned by the Superior Spirits, if you trust them and perform these with all your heart, the Superior Spirits would recognize this to your credit. Conversely, they also recorded your laziness, procrastination or subordination. Brothers and sisters, please understand that every beginning is difficult. If you surmount the difficulty, you are really deserving to be recognized as a hero, a meritorious, determined and virtuous person.

You brothers and sisters who were used to living in comfort, now have to live in ascetic religious life, you have our sympathy. But if you were not poor, you have to learn to be poor, if you were not in misery, you have to learn to be in misery. Thus is the mind of a superior man, as living doesn't need to be comfortable, eating doesn't need to make full. You have to be selfless, to rather take care of the comfort of humanity. This is the duty of the virtuous person.

In this occasion, I would like to plan the ceremony worshipping the Supreme Being. On the 8th day, try to attain merit for two days, celebrate great ceremony with candles and incenses. Try to find a lamp that has sufficient light, because right now we are without. You have a lamp with seven lights. This lamp may be called the seven star lamp. I now give you five minutes for discussion. Take your time to think and respond one by one. (*The séance was stopped momentarily*).

- Are you ready?

(*Answer: The lamp of brother Phối Sư, although old, but may be reclaimed*)

- I said it is temporary, so anything that has seven lights may be used.

(Question: Where should the seven star lamp be hung?)

Right here, to replace this lamp, so you may use it for the séances, but not for regular day. During séances, you need enough light to shine your spirit. You may start at midnight. In evoking superior spirits, you have to have appropriate rituals, with all accoutrements of incense and lights like at this time.

(Question: Do we need to recite the repentance prayer or any other prayer?)

- The Great Senior Immortal announced that he has asked The Supreme Being to come to the séances on the day of great ceremony. On the next day you should recite regular prayers like during spring. In the prayer for relieving sufferings, instead of reciting "saving me" you should recite "saving all living beings." When the Supreme Being comes, do not pray for anything, and do not scurry around. Assign a person to attend the bell. That person shall announce his/her name and then attend the bell. *(Question: Do we attend the bell after prostration?)*

- After you announce your name, the séance will stop, then you attend the bell. When the Supreme Being leaves, all of you should prostrate to bid farewell. Then, evoke the Mother Goddess. The Immortals and Buddhas convey the wishes for the New Year to you all. You all should hang firm to the trunk, to prevent the storm from blowing you away. Whatever the storm is, try to hang firm to the trunk.

Understand? I wish you all a good year.

Good bye.

Ascension.

Saigon, September 12th, 1926, the 6th day of the 8th month of the year Bính Dần.

YOUR MASTER,

Greetings to all of you, children,

When you are successful, don't be hasty to express joy. When you fail, don't be hasty in your sorrow. Sorrow and joy often follow each other or are experienced simultaneously. What you encounter is because it has to be so. Don't be so indignant as to act against My Holy Will. Try to follow this poem to adapt yourself toward a faithful path:

From now on try to follow the Tao with your whole heart.
Accept that the religious path is full of hardship.
God recognizes your sincerity,
The world would admire your bright example.
Your elders have already endeavored to clear obstacles from the path
So that future generations may benefit.
From now on, detach yourself from secular vicissitudes,
Persevering in saving humanity becomes your good meritorious legacy.

September 30th, 1926

JADE EMPEROR, or CAODAI, TEACHING THE TAO IN THE SOUTHERN QUARTER

Greetings to all disciples and guests,

M...N...If there is no important issue, try not to bother the Superior Spirits, who all have their own responsibility, you understand! Be cautious and pay them respect. I am the Superior Being with immense generosity and I forgive your mistakes. However, the Superior Spirits would strictly apply the divine laws to discipline you, so you obey!

Do you understand this poem?

Mr. Hạng Trọng Sơn paid the spring for his horse to drink water.

He was blessed and met with good fortune.

Young generations do not have much trust, but a lot of arguments.

People who deal with others with sincerity will receive respect in return.

Tell Me what you understand!

Guests, please be seated.

(M...N... explained wrongly the poem)

No, it is not so, child. Do you understand these two following verses?

Mr. Lưu Khoan of the Han Dynasty punished criminals by lashings just for them to feel the insult.

Mr. Hạng Trọng Sơn was so pure, he even paid the spring for his horse to drink water.

He did not use for the taking what belongs to nature! You understand!

I like you to teach your family rightly, treat people with pure conscience even for petty matters. Try to read and explain My Holy Teachings to people. Justice and sincerity are My favorite virtues.

Ascension.

Giác Hải Pagoda, Saigon, the 15th day of the 8th month of the year Bính Dần (September 21, 1926).

Sakya Muni Buddha or Cao Dai Tien Ong Dai Bo Tat Ma Ha Tat embodying Buddhism in the Southern Quarter.

Như Nhãn, listen to your Master,

When incarnated as the Buddha, I had four disciples who all denied Me.

When incarnated to found Taoism, I had the disciple Nguơn Thỉ.

When I founded Christianity, I had 12 disciples. But when I was arrested and executed, they all ran away and even sold my body.

And presently, I have gathered quite a few disciples for you. Don't be discouraged. I used to lament that if the Tao was established one day late, there would be one more day of damage for humanity. But divine arrangement was for evils to disturb the path of right and promote evil. This happened to all previous Immortals and Buddhas. Now, humans have conflict with each other because of high positions. You should rely on your buddha heart to se all of living beings'suffering and constantly reincarnating. You should think of Me when you bear this shame. Your merciful behavior makes you deserve to be My child.

If I use My supreme power to interfere, there would be no more divine justice. You should proceed to establish the religious laws and try to save human beings.

Beloved daughter Lâm, if I had to blame someone, I would say that you have delayed the expansion of the Tao and created obstacles. Do you understand why?

Because of the twisted words of the women!

You all have to try your best. I am always by your side. No one could harm the Tao.

Như Nhãn, remember My prediction. Read again the Holy Teachings.

Ascension.

The 9th day of the 9th month of the year Bính Dần (October 15, 1926)

YOUR MASTER,

Listen children,

 I have often said that you rather err and offend Me, as I would forgive you out of love. But you should not offend Angels, Saints, Immortals and Buddhas because they are not so quick to forgive.
 I also said: "Anytime, I came to the séance, I was escorted by innumerable Angels, Saints, Immortals, Buddhas." If you could see with your naked eyes, you would be terrified. But because you did not see and did not know, your mistake may be considered less serious.
 Lack of respect is a serious mistake as judged by the Superior Spirits. I would have to leave to avoid your being punished. I do not mind because of My love. I am just afraid for you to offend the Superior Spirits.

 Ascension.

The 7th day of the 10th month of the year Bính Dần (November 11, 1926)

JADE EMPEROR, or CAODAI, TEACHING THE TAO IN THE SOUTHERN QUARTER.

Greetings to all disciples, all beloved daughters, all guests,

Ng…, listen to Me:
Your legacy has been blessed.
Your merits in saving living beings will be rewarded.
Look at previous examples of wisdom
To cultivate your virtues in order to return to your position in Nirvana.

You two have the heart to build up the Tao. Keep enduring the hardships in accomplishing your task. Honors and wealth are like drops of dew on the lawn or floating clouds in the wind. Your virtues are the best way to guide you on the road back to Nirvana, and to avoid reincarnation. Because of love for life, I did not flout My Supreme Position, and came to found the Third Universal Salvation to save humanity from the ocean of sufferings. Whoever recognizes the Tao will be blessed. Whoever doesn't will be reincarnated in suffering. Hurry to return to the Tao. If you remain seduced by secular attractions, it would be too late to repent. Alas! I have established the divine laws according to the divine justice. I am heartbroken to see living beings led astray by evil, but I cannot bend the universal law. Therefore, the Third Universal Salvation is like a school to earn credits. If you repent and embark upon the bright path and cultivate your hearts and your virtues, you will reunite with Me at the end. People should try to listen to Me and always self re-evaluate often.

Holy Message on the opening day.

November 18 1926 (the 14th day of the 10th month of the year Bính Dần)

Gò Kén pagoda Tây Ninh (Từ Lâm pagoda)

JADE EMPEROR, or CAODAI, TEACHING THE TAO IN THE SOUTHERN QUARTER.

Greetings to all disciples and all beloved daughters.
Female disciples, listen.

The perfumed heart wafts its fragrance from earth to sky.
Self-cultivation enlightens, guiding all souls by and by.
Pray to Buddha Quan Yin (Goddess of Mercy) *for all of your life,*
And hold up the Tao in unending light.

Daughter Lâm appointed as Giáo Sư, divinely named as Hương Thanh,

Daughter Ca appointed as Phó Giáo Sư, divinely named as Hương Ca,

Daughter Đường already appointed, keep the same position.

Other daughters, wait for the next meeting when there are more disciples and I will appoint all of you at the same time.

I bless you all. Perform the rituals as instructed.

Ascension.

The 4th day of the 11th month of the year Bính Dần
(December 8, 1926)

JADE EMPEROR, or CAODAI, TEACHING THE TAO IN THE SOUTHERN QUARTER.

To all disciples, all beloved daughters, all guests, Listen to Me

Your feet are unaccustomed to the long new road.
Though you have cultivated your virtues well,
You are like blooming bushes awaiting the spring
Or the brightly colored lotus bud craving summer,
The Holy Water washes away all secular desires
The Holy Teachings lead you to immortality
You are blessed to be alive at the Third Salvation
Hasten your steps toward the meditating woods.

From now on, I am your leader to guide you on the path of virtues, I am always at your side, you have only to wait for My orders. The road is long and full of obstacles, but you will be able to surmount all dangers to meet Me at the end. Some disciples don't have enough faith, and are ready to give up easily while meeting difficulties. According to the divine arrangement of the Three Religions, the Third Universal Salvation of the great way was founded in the South to save all living beings from suffering. It is miraculous, at times visible, at times invisible depending on divine mechanism.

The presence of the Tao in a country means that disasters of this country are about to end. You must purify your heart, follow the examples of suffering overcome by love and help each other like children of the same family. This would lead you to Nirvana, avoiding this suffering world.

Try to understand.
Ascension.

The 7th day of the 11th month of the year Bính Dần (December 11, 1926)

JADE EMPEROR, or CAODAI, TEACHING THE TAO IN THE SOUTHERN QUARTER.

To all disciples, all beloved daughters, all guests,

T..., My gentle disciple, listen to Me:

Conservation of noble teachings is no poverty but an art.

It can be a helpful companion to walk safely on the religious path.

Realization of the Tao in your heart would be an invaluable assistance

Like the flowered apricot bough to lead you out of this secular world.

You have been blessed to meet Me to guide you on the miraculous religious path at this late time of your life. I have ordered Superior Spirits to help you in your duty of guiding living beings imminently, so that you may complete your mission at the end of your life. You should be perseverant and truthful to deserve the noble position when you return to Me. Try to pay attention to this. The happiest days of living beings have gone; disaster awaits! People of the world are still dispersing suffering and sorrow to others by their cruelty. Disasters from the East and the West, according to divine arrangement, will take turns to destroy the inhumane, leading to turmoil in the world. Because of love, I created the Third Universal Salvation to save blessed living beings from suffering and punishment. Whoever blessed would recognize and follow the path, whoever unfortunate, would fall into evil hands.

Alas! Millions of people have floundered in the midst of the river of sufferings, and the life boats can save only a few, because virtuous people are rare, and useless people are so numerous. Good traditions are deteriorating, religious rules are wildly violated. Incompetent and non virtuous people use all maneuvers to rise to the top. Holy teachings are divinely arranged to be followed by people who cultivate self and maintain good human traditions. They may reach immortality. Living beings must be cautious toward people who care only for secular life and denounce holy teachings.

Tr..., you should read briefly the last holy teachings to living beings and tell them to repent before evoking Me. Ascension.

The 8th day of the 11th month of the year Bính Dần
(December 12, 1926)

JADE EMPEROR, or CAODAI, TEACHING THE TAO IN THE SOUTHERN QUARTER

To all disciples and all beloved daughters.
T..., would you two, husband and wife, follow Me with sincerity and respect until the end?
In this suffering world, it is difficult to avoid mistakes even for highly virtuous persons.

But repentance is always invaluable. Immortals and Buddhas of ancient times have reached noble divine positions thanks to repentance. Exposed to secular life with wealth, honors, fighting, sufferings, people would realize that life is just a dream, a karmic show, not permanent. They then may find paths to self-cultivation. If I use you two to build up the congregation to save living beings, would you have faithfulness, endurance and patience in the service for humanity?

T...child, when the Tao is founded, the responsibility to save living being is reserved for predestined persons.

If there were not obstacles arranged by the divine mechanism, the Tao would be spread all over the world within one year. But the real and the unreal are mixed together. Only your virtues will allow you to surmount the difficulties. I have endured many hardships to guide you. But many of you abuse the situation, offend Me and oppress disciples. If not because of love, I would not found the Tao to save holy souls and people who have floundered in the ocean of sufferings alike, and I would instead erase all of them.

You have time to think, I give you more time to contemplate in order to attain perfect virtues. At that time, you beloved daughter would become My hands in the salvation of human beings. I have some words for the two of you:

You guide one another's steps toward freedom
You have each other for support
You come together thanks to good fortune,
And become husband and wife by destiny.
Day by day, time passes and,
Facing the long road ahead, you may falter.

Follow the example of Mr. Trương, who refused wealth and honors from the Hớn dynasty,

In order to live a life of wisdom.

Listen and contemplate.

I bless you all.

Ascension.

14-12-1926

December 14th 1926

JADE EMPEROR, or CAODAI, TEACHING THE TAO IN THE SOUTHERN QUARTER

Greetings to all disciples, beloved daughters and guests, Th…, listen to Me child:

> *If you wish for tranquility at the end of your days,*
> *You have to teach and guide living beings here below.*
> *Immortality demands strife*
> *Along the secular way.*
> *Remain faithful,*
> *Though poor with no honors bestowed,*
> *The legacy you leave is but your good name.*
> *In spring, cut the flowering apricot bough.*

From this day forward, I hold the power in the world; I lead you to Nirvana. Cultivate your virtues, teach living beings who are still in their secular dream. Try to change your profane heart, so your virtues would be refined. Services to humanity are tiring but need to be accomplished to attain noble divine positions. For the sake of living beings, endure hardship, drop all frivolous positions and honors of this world, surmount all difficult obstacles, cultivate your virtues. Some day, you will reach eternal happiness, avoid further suffering incarnations and enjoy immortality. Try to listen and plan your journey accordingly.

You guests should also correct yourself, have good heart and sincerity to attain approval from the Superior Spirits.

For the love of life, I have accepted many non virtuous people to give them opportunities to repent. If they continue in their cruelty and if I do not use My compassion to found the Tao, they would be punished by the Superior Spirits.

Being submerged in the ocean of suffering, not reaching to grasp for the saving willow branch, not aspiring to escape from reincarnation, but instead committing more crimes, you will be totally responsible for your actions. It would be too late to repent.

Ascension.

January 3, 1927

JADE EMPEROR, or CAODAI, TEACHING THE TAO IN THE SOUTHERN QUARTER

Greetings to all disciples, beloved daughters and all living beings.

All living beings, listen:
The Third Universal Salvation of the Great Way, according to the divine laws, gathers the three religions, opens widely the Tao to guide humanity to Nirvana to avoid reincarnation. It uses the holy heart to help humanity to accomplish their responsibility in this world of suffering.

Alas! Few persons bother to look for the holy way but many rush toward the evil way. They carry their heavy physical body, are busy with secular attractions, honor and wealth, compete with each other, neglect the religious rules of the precious Tao, thus leading themselves to the abyss. Many use their powerful influence to compete and fight against each other and forget their responsibility and karmic debt.

The more intense the fighting, the closer is the destruction. The blessed people realize the divine path, rowing their boat to isolated places of quietude, washing off their worldly dust, purifying and cultivating their inner self, aim for a nobler position and escape reincarnation. Others following their evil heart, run after personal interests, become floundered in the ocean of sufferings without repentance which would allow them to avoid disastrous punishment. The divine road is tortuous, your secular steps are still hesitant, without self-evaluation to realign your stride, you would fall to the wayside. Try to understand.
Ascension.

January 8th, 1927

JADE EMPEROR, or CAODAI, TEACHING THE TAO IN THE SOUTHERN QUARTER

Greetings to all disciples, beloved daughters and guests. C... listen to Me:

The golds of fall have donned their wintry mantle;
Self-reflection brings the contentment of Virtue.
Orioles sing in the pines upon the mountain.
Hark; one still yearns to come upon the forest crane.
Stepping gingerly to avoid the path of worldly aims,
The pure spring rinsing away all earthly defilement,
A bright, shining soul lights the distant shore for those who follow.

I recognize your righteous heart. Continue to withstand sufferings in order to guide living beings in the right path of escaping reincarnation. You are born at a time when non virtuous people depart from religious rules and are engulfed in disasters. They are confused and become submerged in the ocean of sufferings. They do not cultivate their virtues, but on the contrary, commit more crimes. If the Merciful does not found the Third Universal Salvation to save the predestined souls, the whole world would be destroyed and even incarnated Saints and Immortals may have difficulties in regaining their position. Disaster looms from the East to the West. Divine rules will punish the criminals and the world will be desolate. If your steps are still hesitant, if you do not reevaluate self soon enough, the lifeboat will fade away with the tide. When the Holy Water has receded, then it would be too late to repent. Try to understand and listen, living beings!
Ascension.

January 21st 1927

JADE EMPEROR, or CAODAI, TEACHING THE TAO IN THE SOUTHERN QUARTER.

Greetings to all disciples, beloved daughters and guests.

The way to Immortality and Buddhahood is always waiting for predestined, blessed persons to cultivate self, serve humanity and escape from this world of confusion.

People are still running after desires and floundering in the ocean of sufferings. The judgment palace has tried many criminals, and yet people are still launching into lives of crime. Worldly life is but a short dream. Being born to this world, one becomes an exile sailing upon the ocean of sufferings in order to fulfill one's human duties and pay off karmic debt. People have endured all forms of misery, gone from laughing to crying on their worldly path, without ever awakening. Chaos has trumped religious rules, good traditions deteriorated, people fought and competed with each other causing division among religions. Thus, it became difficult to distinguish between righteousness and evil. People could not stop their cruelty until their last breath. No wonder why they were exiled into hell.

The Tao was founded to guide people back from the suffering world and on to their destiny, but if they do not hurry to heed the Tao, their ephemeral life will flow away as surely as life's blood. Try to understand!

Ascension.

January 22nd, 1927

JADE EMPEROR, or CAODAI, TEACHING THE TAO IN THE SOUTHERN QUARTER.

Tr..., My gentle disciple, Trương, I have sanctified the religious dress for you, you are allowed to wear it to attend ceremony. N..., wait for your dress to be finished, I will then sanctify it.

Th..., listen to Me:
Showered by My blessings,
The holy way sets every step right.
Nirvana is waiting for you,
Along the Vị river under the moonlight,
On the Tần mountain, clothed by its dew and clouds,
You're cleansed of desires,
Neither seeking wealth, nor proud.
Living a fully spiritual life,
You are an exemplar of sincerity,
Away from a confused and suffering world
You have set your ship to sea.

Tr..., I am pleased to have beloved disciples like you in this holy land. You should expect the road to be beset with difficulties and obstacles, and without leisure.

Being born as human, you must endeavor to fulfill your special responsibility in order to pay off your karmic debt and to attain a position, which is much nobler than the frivolous titles of this chaotic world.

Though time has flown away and life has been tainted with misery, your worldly desires and ambitions are endless. You flounder in a sea of ephemeral honors and wealth with all kind of temporal attractions.

All the misery of life only leads you people to deserted tombs.

If you would only discover the miraculous Tao, live a religious life, cultivate your virtues, and guide living beings, you may find immortality in Nirvana and escape reincarnation.

Try to find the way before it's too late.
Try to understand, living beings.
Ascension.

The 20th day of the 12th month of the year of the Yang Fire Tiger
January 23, 1927

JADE EMPEROR, or CAODAI, TEACHING THE TAO IN THE SOUTHERN QUARTER.

To all disciples and beloved daughters.
CH.., listen to Me:

The mountain pines are highly fragrant,
The Tao will reunite human family upon one path.
You must walk along life's long road
To hear the music of the holy mountain.
Then you will realize the way home,
And enjoy a holy life among the mountain pines.
In finding your way to immortality,
You will leave a good example for posterity.

I just want to let you know that the Tao will bring your family to a common path where a peaceful and contented life is much better than the earthly one, with its wealth and honors. The best happiness is the great family reunion.
I bless you all.
Ascension.

The 20th day of the 12th month of the year of the Yang Fire Tiger
January 23, 1927

JADE EMPEROR, or CAO DAI, TEACHING THE TAO IN THE SOUTHERN QUARTER

Greetings to all disciples and all beloved daughters:
The sun is setting in the meditation forest of Mount Tần.
Your suffering in now done.
With perseverance, you cultivate self in the Holy way,
And still try to serve humanity.
With Guidance, wild geese return to the bamboo grove,
Their wings set aloft from this earthly shore.
Even as time goes by, turning your hair gray,
You will be blessed as you guide living beings in the Way.

Time is as relentless as the waning moon: just so, you age with the moon's waxing and waning. If you are not mindful in following the right way to escape the world of confusion, your karmic debt may never be paid.

You seek a quiet spring on a high mountain to wash away earthly debris. Use the Tao as a ladder to advance to the highest noble position and to avoid sin.

There is truly punishment and reward that you will realize.

I bless you all.

Ascension.

The 20th day of the 12th month of the year of the Yang Fire Tiger (January 23, 1927)

JADE EMPEROR, or CAO DAI, TEACHING THE TAO IN THE SOUTHERN QUARTER

Greetings to all disciples and all beloved daughters: N..., listen to Me:

At the Lake Động Đình, if you claim your birthright,
You will realize the Tao at a ripe age.
You have passed the test for becoming a sage,
And used your lifetime to walk the Holy way
To reach immortality.
You are now at the decline of years,
After enduring the vicissitudes and challenges of secular strife.
You have to gain merit by serving humanity
Even while enduring suffering trying to escape this earthly life.

I have sent Immortals and Buddhas to utilize miracles to guide you to the spiritual life and to use the Tao as a ladder leading you back to your original (spiritual) position.

I have revealed the divine process to Th., try to learn and discipline yourself by this example.

It is not uncommon to see many Saints incarnated to this earth of misery, and, immersed in the world of confusion, seduced by worldly entertainments, also forget about the Tao and become lost on their way back to their lofty positions. Then it is difficult for the Bát Nhã lifeboat to save them.

Be patient, maintain your virtue, be good moral examples for future generations, earn merit by serving humanity so that at the end of your life, through the Tri-religion Court, you will be able to return to your spiritual origins with a good heart, completely detached from this world of misery. You must anticipate your family situation and strive in the Tao. You must also be present at the holy temple at the time of amendment of the bylaws.

Later, you will hold the power from the Tao to guide humanity here where I have many beloved disciples.

I bless you all, children.

I ascend.

The 20th day of the 12th month of the year of the Yang Fire Tiger (January 23, 1927)

JADE EMPEROR, or CAO DAI, TEACHING THE TAO IN THE SOUTHERN QUARTER

Greetings to all disciples and all beloved daughters:

H., listen to Me:

Upon the ocean, you are sailing in the good wind,
You are heading the right way, toward the Holy Tao.
You were immersed in filthy secular seductions
But now you can wash away your sufferings in the Perfume River.
The mandarin life was dimmed by the fog of forgetting,
Yet the moonlight illumines the road of remembrance:
Cultivate your virtues to guide humanity
To the road of immortality.

As time passes, the guests of this Earth suffer much. Could any of them manage to carry along all earthly honors to the Afterworld in order to reach nobler positions? Your time is almost over. Try to cultivate yourself in order to reach Nirvana.

I congratulate you for your sincerity and respect. Try to guide humanity, and you will reach your noble position in the end.

I bless your family.
I bless you all.
I ascend.

Tây Ninh, (Gò kén Pagoda) the 12th day of the 1st month of the year Đinh Mão (February 13, 1927)

JADE EMPEROR or CAODAI TEACHING THE TAO IN THE SOUTHERN QUARTER

When I founded the Great Way in the southern part of this country, my intent was to compensate a country which has been greatly affected by My rage. Thus I forgave and rewarded your country in such an honorable way that humans have never seen before; no other country of the 68th planet could have! For that reward, there would be no reason for you to have less privilege than other countries. Alas! What a tragedy! What a pain! You've been so arrogant that you have despised this Great Tao, this most beautiful and precious pearl! I am tired of seeing such a way of practicing the Tao by some of the females. Thus many times I've been sad and become angry and did not want to create the female college. But you are all My children, whether male or female. I did not have the heart to abandon you. Because I love you all very much, I had used rebuke and advice to guide you (e.g., the female Cardinal Lâm Hương Thanh) back to your initial position. Also, because it was My promise to the Quan Âm (Kwan Yin, Female Boddhisattva, Goddess of Mercy) so that I reserve the privilege for you to use your service as proof of repentance. Dear child! I am heartbroken to see you suffer. I do not want to see you lost forever just because of mistake.

Do you see how much I love you? I maintained the female college just for you, but they did not come when I called. They did not listen when I taught. Yet I did not have the heart to punish them as severely as they deserved.

I founded the Tao based on the principle "HARMONY." You are the eldest sister, use your judgment.
Call whomever you think is deserving for Me to teach. Tr...! You should help your younger sisters! Obey.

I ascend.

The 18th day of the 1st month of the year Đinh Mão (year of the cat)
February 19, 1927

Quan Thánh Đế Quân
Greetings to all disciples, all sisters and living beings.
The eyes of wisdom illuminate the universe,
With holy virtues, I care to maintain
Vietnam in prosperity and peace,
And to open the Tao's gate unto the world.

Quan Âm, Buddhisattva of the South Sea:
Greetings to all disciples, all sisters, and all living beings.

The primordial faith in the South saves living beings,
Using the holy virtues to change the world's situation.
Pray for divine blessings to defuse all disaster,
In meditation, use the Yin wind to find peace within your heart, And you will reach wisdom.

Lý Thái Bạch:
Greetings to all disciples, all sisters, and all living beings.

The Tao is open to the South, bringing harmony and prosperity,
The white star of the divine light shines into people's hearts.
Connect your hearts together for the future generations,
And lead the way to the Cloud Palace.

Living beings, be in deep meditation in order to meet the Great Mercy.

The 18th day of the 1st month of the year Đinh Mão (year of the cat) February 19, 1927

JADE EMPEROR, or CAO DAI, TEACHING THE TAO IN THE SOUTHERN QUARTER

Greetings to all disciples, all beloved daughters and all guests.

I am happy for you disciples here who have sincerity and respect and the heart of guiding humanity to the right path.

Being one day late in founding the Tao would leave millions of human beings lost in sin. I therefore want each of you to put all your heart into spreading the Tao.

What makes Me most happy is your mutual love and assistance, mutual sharing of happiness and misery, and mutual guiding and supporting each other on the road to the Tao, like brothers and sisters from one family, in order to escape from this earthly shore of chaos and struggles where millions of souls are immersed in the seduction of materiality, power, and honor.

I command that you should not lose your grasp on mutual love because of petty earthly matters; that is not the behavior of virtuous persons.

I ascend.

The 19th day of the first month of the year Đinh Mão
February 20, 1927

JADE EMPEROR, or CAO DAI, TEACHING THE TAO IN THE SOUTHERN QUARTER

Greetings to all disciples, all beloved daughters.
Listen, all living beings.

The Tao of God has been established three times, saving millions of souls. You should take care to step in the right direction to realize the miraculous mechanism of these revelations.

The Creator has already arranged to guide and bless all living beings during this last era.

Great Spirits, because of justice, have assisted and saved predestined people from sinful downfall. You should be aware of this situation and follow the guiding light to the road of wisdom and find the quiet spring of the holy mountain to wash off the earthly debris of confusion.

Out of love, I meet with the Three Religions, sprinkling holy water out into the universe to save incarnated higher souls before Judgment Day. Misery and disasters from East to West, according to divine arrangement, will befall cruel countries that have generated animosities in this world.

Whoever hurries to step onto the right path to serve humanity and build up divine merit to counteract karma will avoid future sorrow. Living beings, try to understand.

I ascend.

The 20th day of the first month of the year Đinh Mão
February 21, 1927

JADE EMPEROR, or CAO DAI, TEACHING THE TAO IN THE SOUTHERN QUARTER

Greetings to all disciples, all beloved daughters, and all living beings.

I am happy for you for meriting blessings to find the right path. You have to work cooperatively with one another to walk the road to eternity. Although you cannot see it, you may reach your ultimate destiny if you come to realize the principle of the Tao that I have carefully taught you. If you could achieve more enthusiasm for the Tao, you would reach it sooner than you imagine. That blissful dimension is not far away. It is right here on this planet, though it alludes you because you have been occupied with life's base attractions and forgetting the noble way.

You must know that in this universe, human beings are My precious children and I take time to care for all of you, making sure that you will repent and ultimately enjoy My blessings.

I ask you: Would that be your intention?

Tr..., relate this to all your younger brothers and sisters!

I ascend.

Tayninh (Gò Kén pagoda), the 27th of the 1st month of the year Đinh Mão (2-28-1927)

Here is THAI BACH

Greetings to all disciples and all sisters.

Bính Thanh, the figure of the Buddha Gautama Sakya Muni in front of the Hiệp Thiên Đài (Heavenly Union Palace) needs to be handled with care. The Supreme Being has sanctified it. Take the same precaution for the Universal Globe during its dissembling or assembling. After taking it apart, you need to evoke me so I can guard it for the time before you lay your hands back upon it.

As for the new temples, remind disciples to pray to the Supreme Being to sanctify them. Besides, a temporary temple has to be built on the empty lot. The temporary Hiệp Thiên Đài has to be built in front. You disciples must clear the forest in front of this lot. Place a stake at the center, then at the Cà Na Pond, place another stake 50m away from the first one. The Holy See is to be built between these two stakes. Remember to measure 27m from the first stake toward the Cà Na Pond where you will build the Bát Quái Đài (Octagonal Palace) in the square of 27m wide. It needs to have an octagonal shape with an 8-sided roof. The elevation of the floor should be nine meters. The height of the Bát Quái Đài is also nine meters. Place a blue light on the top of the Bát Quái Đài. Next to the Bát Quái Đài is the main temple, to be 81m long and 27m wide. I will sketch it for you. On both sides of the Hiệp Thiên Đài are the two towers: The Lôi Âm Cổ Đài (tower for the Thunder Drum) on the right, and the Bạch Ngọc Chung Đài (tower for the White Pearl Bell) on the left.

This afternoon, Hộ Pháp, and Thượng Phẩm must put a pen at the end of the corbeille à bec and provide a large piece of paper. Then evoke me so that I can draw. Bính Thanh must also be there. Besides them, no one else is allowed to be in the temple. Obey.

And you have to purchase the piece of land at Cà Na Pond for future use as Động Đình Lake.
Obey.
I ascend.

March 2, 1927.

This is LY BACH

Greetings to all disciples and all sisters.

Disciples, this is a difficult time for spiritual travelers. In order to surmount difficulties, you must have perseverance and dedication and try to put your virtues above all other desires on this Earth. The Tao is about to embark. You just need to embrace the challenges, which are like a final test for you. The spreading of the Tao has been predestined by the divine mechanism, which will always prevail over human efforts. I just try to let you know that you have to pay attention to your work. The road is full of difficulties but you have the divine guiding light, which will assist you in reaching your goal.

The three religions are meeting with the Great Mercy to plan for the establishment of the Tao everywhere on this planet according to divine will in this final era.

I ascend.

March 3, 1927.

JADE EMPEROR, or CAODAI, TEACHING THE TAO IN THE SOUTHERN QUARTER

Greetings to all disciples, all beloved daughters, and all guests.

Although the Tao has dispersed its blessing to all living beings, people are still mired in their earthly dream. People have not been able to escape secular seductions; done too few good deeds and too many evil ones; too little of merit but too much of crime. Nevertheless, these things have just happened according to divine arrangement.

I love you all equally, but many of you have to pay your karma. I am heartbroken when I have to uphold justice according to the divine mechanism. What you need to do is to keep following your path, using your merit to surmount obstacles, to wash off earthly silt, in order to reach Eternity. Very few people can surrender to the saffron robe and live a monk's life in order to escape from the turmoil and confusion of a world where honors, power, and wealth are perceived as lofty. How sad! What a regret!

There is no wind blowing into your sail. The wild geese keep returning to their old familiar places. The path of the Tao is nearly forgotten and covered with the moss of neglect. But then, as you begin your spiritual journey, no one can say if this is a blessing or a misfortune!

I ascend.

March 3, 1927.

YOUR MASTER, children!

I want to inform you clearly.

You have progressed quite well on the road to the Tao. In order to complete your responsibility you have to surmount difficulties to reach your noble goal. Most of you have put your hearts and mind into the effort because you respect Me and because you want to save humanity. But many of you have also used an evil heart, creating turmoil and hatred at the gate of the Tao.

I have the mercy and the love of life to guide you. I would not treat you unequally. I would not use your own evil actions to hurt you. You are children of one same family and are treated equally. However, I would pay more attention to the weak. Many times I intended--but did not have the heart--to punish the ones who abused their positions and titles to create turmoil in the Tao. However, the Saints and Angels have recorded all their actions and will discipline them at the end. There are many hypocrites. You could not trust anyone more than yourselves. Many have come to the Tao just for the opportunity to discover important secret matters. The miraculous mechanism was already arranged in the divine book. The Tao was opened with the goal to guide predestined persons to traverse the difficult road to return to Me. It's totally up to you to reach your goal.

I could not tell you all about the divine mechanism. Tr., T., H., have almost completed their duties and their karma. That's why there was such an incident; otherwise, they could not avoid greater disaster. It was that I wanted to save them.

I have implemented the spirit of safety and peace in creating the Tao. In the past, many times humans shed blood for the Tao without success.

That's why I have to expose you to all the sorrows of the road to the Tao, so that you may gain experience and be successful.

M., N., S..., from now on, you don't have to attend routinely such a session like the last one if there was no issue that involves you, because it would only waste your time. I have sketched out the trail for you to follow. You don't have to worry. Because even if you try to go too fast, you couldn't reach the goal sooner; and even if you were to slow down, it would still not delay your journey. All progress flows from Me. All difficulties are just to make you work a little harder. If all disciples are of the same heart as you, the road to the Tao would be very joyful and nothing could break your spirit. You have to think about it.

S: reported about T.M.

Alas! Money, good food, and prized possessions have seduced ordinary men. But take heart! I would not use such a person in promoting the Tao. Even ordinary men would not use ill gotten gains. Look at examples of old stories. If Hàn Tín had not betrayed his friend, he would not have died suddenly, seemingly without reason. In the example of Trương Tử Phòng, if Phạm Tăng did not do things against God's will, all karma would be resolved instantly.

I have said you should work harder in order to surmount those difficulties.

Try to understand.

I ascend.

5-3-1927

Quan Âm, Boddhisattva of the South Sea.

Greetings to all disciples, all sisters, and all living beings.
Dignitaries, be seated.

Listen, younger sisters.
I have the honor to witness your respect. You have to cooperate with each other in order to guide future generations. Many sisters have not put all their heart into the Tao. You have to try harder to deserve the love of the Supreme Being and to be proud as Vietnamese women. You will not miss out on your rewards, but time is running out, if you delay you may lose track. I am glad you have labored in completing your responsibilities, which I have been expecting from you all.

Take heed of exemplary women of the South,
You will join together as in one family home.
Women shall guide one another in the Way,
Mirroring goddesses upon lotus throne.

Please take heed, disciples and sisters.
I ascend.

March 5, 1927

JADE EMPEROR OR CAODAI TEACHING THE TAO IN THE SOUTHERN QUARTER

Greeting to disciples, to beloved female disciples, and guests.
K... Listen to Me.

In the field of meditation, the noon bell chimes soon,
Hurry back to Me as is your fortune.
Virtue like moonlight illumines
The fallow field lit by color in autumn.
Life's flowered apricot wilts in the snow,
Evil dies but Virtue rises to the Tao.
On this path, gentleness is borne,
And you will return to your spiritual home.

The sky rises above all aspects of life. The holy way is leading every worldly step. There are many changes at the end of this last era. This 68th planet has suddenly received a sacred light to awaken people, shining the way to save predestined people and protecting them from being destroyed by the cruelty of humanity. Many people have foundered in the ocean of sufferings, painting a sad picture of human life, where humanity could neither balance good and bad deeds nor pay attention to karmic laws. Forests and mountains of their homeland are waiting for them to return, but they are still lost in the abyss, their desperate calls for help unheard. All previous credits of love and service to humanity, all holy teachings of sages and saints are washed away during the one hundred year of life's games. If there were no miraculous way to remind humanity to self-cultivate, they would still be fighting and killing each other for materiality until the end, in which there would be no more human traces.

The way of God has shone forth. People should try to wake up. Life is not long enough for them to be idle. In the school of life, people should balance the blessings and karma, and cultivate self before it is too late. Human beings, try to understand.

I always want you to get together to open the good path, to love and help each other, to share your joy and your sufferings, while guiding humanity. If because of secular ambition, you become divided, hating and fighting each other, you would make poor examples to future generations, and the great way would therefore be preempted. Paying attention to My words would be a great sincere and respectful gift to Me.

I bless you all.

Ascension.

The 4th day of the second month of the year Đinh Mão (March 7, 1927)

JADE EMPEROR OR CAODAI TEACHING THE TAO IN THE SOUTHERN QUARTER

Greeting to all disciples, to beloved female disciples, and guests.

Disciples, listen to Me.

Over more than one long year, you have undergone many hardships in trying to promote the Great Way that I have founded because of My love for humanity, who face drowning in the ocean of suffering because of Karma. I hold the secret miraculous mechanism powered by justice to move the universe, and therefore life has to evolve in cycles so that the process of purification would lead to the perfection of humanity and the transformation of the Earth into Heaven. Evils would be destroyed, gentle people would ascend to heaven; the strong but evil people would be vanquished while meek and virtuous people would triumph. If the Tao were not created, people, because of their cruelty, would reincarnate again and again to pay their karma, and no one would know when this earth would be fully blessed and the profane would evolve to salvation.

School is almost out and you get to deal with some difficult tests. Most of you have some credits of serving humanity, but the outcomes are still uncertain. You did not show good examples of virtue and love as I have arranged. I have said: "The divine machine has to change according to your virtues, and therefore I had to modify the miraculous mechanism using love and peace to lead you in your cultivation. Previously, humanity had many times undergone hardships and self-sacrifice for the Tao, but because of their uncertainty together with many vicissitudes of life, brotherhood among humanity has not been realized."

Cruel people have used their secular force to disturb the progression of the Tao. Though the chaos and sufferings of the human community were bound to happen, your service to humanity and your virtues should not delay in shining the way for future generations to follow to reach Nirvana. I therefore have modified your steps, creating joy, gentleness, and enthusiasm, instead of sorrow, worries, difficulties and discouragement for you to overcome. Although this would lessen some of your merit and therefore your rewards, peace is bestowed to all humanity. Do you understand that divine mechanism?

Tr..., try to understand. So too, you other disciples.

The most important issue you all have to pay attention to is to take care of the holy house. Each of you has to bring in a little effort, and your name and your good example would be remembered by future generations. Try to understand.

Tr.., people who wish to be initiated should be accepted. Let them know that the New Codes have been established. The Hierarchical Council just needs to implement them.

This would be good for you, your virtues and services.

Ascension.

June 1, 1927 (year Đinh Mão) (PhướcThọ cenacle)

JADE EMPEROR OR CAODAI TEACHING THE TAO IN THE SOUTHERN QUARTER

Greeting to all disciples,

Tr..., since the founding of the Tao, most disciples pay all their sincerity to guide humanity and to promote the Tao. They are the ones I trust to put all their efforts into clearing away the thorns to lead humanity on the divine path to escape from the ocean of sufferings, which is this nonsense planet.

The Tao has been established. Most disciples have cleansed their dirty feet, undergone many hardships to spread the love and to show good examples to future generations. However, the lifeboat, according to the divine mechanism, has left behind many profane people; they are the unfortunate disciples who did not maintain their virtues, and committed evil actions, bespoiling My precious Tao.

You have put all your intention into the Tao, and many times have undergone hardships, trying to set good examples for future generations to follow to reach Nirvana, the state in which there is only bliss without any worries. Your merit will determine your final destiny. At the end of this 6th month, I will stop all initiation séances, and from then on you have to use only your sincerity and all your accumulated knowledge in order to spread the Tao.

Following are My last words you should heed: Don't worry about evil people, they have their own destiny, you just need to keep climbing the divine ladder toward unification with Me, which is the most precious aspiration of humanity. I allow you to accept initiation of disciples just like at other places.

I bless you all.

Ascension.

September 12, 1927

LY BACH

Thượng Trung Nhựt, the Great Mercy has given you a great responsibility of spreading the Tao, in collaboration with the Sacerdotal Council, to find the way to lead dignitaries and disciples in their activities and practices. You have to be just with all your sincerity to interact with disciples without disappointing them. Everything was arranged by the Great Mercy; you all just need to take time to go forward.

Whoever does not keep up their virtues and cooperate with each other to promote the Tao will be watched by Superior Spirits. Their records will be judged at the end according to divine laws. You should follow the holy teachings of the Great Mercy. You may submit to me the petition of promotion for whoever has closely followed the rules and regulations of the Sacerdotal Council. Whoever has ambition to create another way, leading people into a wrong path, will unfortunately end up at the bottom of the abyss despite all merits of their previous life.

You should prepare well the teaching of the Tao. The local councils as well as each disciple will have their own duty, and shall meet once a month on the full moon evening to discuss local activities, to review rules and regulations so that they would befit the majority of people . Then, the Tao would have the highest and most important value, and you would find satisfaction in moving forward.

At each meeting with the local councils, the three Đầu Sư should be present, as well as the three members of the Hiệp Thiên Đài as witnesses, and the minutes should be well recorded.

Among the disciples, I have to inform you that most female disciples don't have sufficient CaoDai knowledge.

You have to mandate them to be present at the routine worship ceremonies to listen to the sermon so that they could learn together with male disciples. Later, I will choose from among them one capable of giving the sermon to female disciples at a separate worship session.

Tr....: *Please allow monthly worshipping ceremonies in Cholon.*

You have all the right to decide.

From now on, H... will be a member of the Hiệp Thiên Đài.

Those are the recommendations for all. Give your best effort for the Tao. Show your sincerity and respect to the Supreme Being.

Ascension.

September 17, 1927

YOUR MASTER,

Children,

I have said I used peace and gentleness to lead you on the divine way. You should pay attention, put all your mind and your heart to work, and you will certainly progress regardless of obstacles. The only problem is that you are separated from the holy teachings, and are just too busy with secular affairs. The Giáo Hữu should be concerned about the sermon for every major worshipping ceremony. They should have prepared a text of holy teachings to read to all disciples so that they could receive holy teachings to stimulate their progression on the divine way.

So do Tr… and L… Th…, My beloved daughter.

Tr…said: *I have given the topics of the sermon to the Giáo Hữu last night at the ceremony at Cầu Kho temple.*

Good! Any Giáo Hữu who is not up to their duty, and does not listen to My instructions, should be reported to Lý Bạch for proper action.

Tr…: addressed about the printing of holy messages.

Good! But holy messages and poems should be carefully selected and then approved by the Sacerdotal Council before publication.

Children! Most disciples would like to be divinely appointed, but don't understand what it is about. Many Saints, Immortals, and Buddhas, who don't have important karmic debt, when incarnated, just need to practice regularly their cultivation, and they may return to their original positions without the need of divine appointment.

Divine appointment is designed for Saints, Immortals, and Buddhas who have left the world. They have to perform great services to humanity in order to return to their initial positions.

Remember, because of love, I granted you divine appointment, but if dignitaries are concerned more about titles and positions than cultivation of virtues, their punishment would be doubled.

Tr…, L…, Th…, beloved daughters, My three children!

Because of love, this is the last divine appointment for you. Now the rules and regulations have been established, and if you won't follow them, Lý Bạch and Quan Âm would protest. From now on, whoever deserves the function, would be recommended and selected by disciples. Only Lý Bạch can propose a divine appointment. And I will then approve.

Tr..! Try more to interact with the government. There will be support from angels. Don't worry!

I bless you all.

Ascension.

The first day of the 10th month of the year Đinh Mão (1927)

YOUR MASTER.

Children, it has not been too long since the recruiting séances were stopped, and there have been many difficulties. I have trained each of you so that you will have all authority to realize the divine will to lead humanity and to spread the Tao to all the world. The celestial machine has determined to found the Tao to save living beings. If today, at this time, the Tao could not be perfectly established, when would it be? How many of you would have enough divine credit to reach unification with Me? I have revealed a little about that issue. Try to find out and understand. Don't misunderstand that the Tao spontaneously becomes prosperous and leads you automatically to the liberation no matter what your virtues. Whether you fail or succeed, I would wait until the end to judge on your accomplished work. I have foretold to you about the worldly chaos, which has begun to spread. If your skills are not sharpened with great virtue, peaceful cooperation, complete modesty and harmony among each other, the Tao would become a tangled mockery, which would be difficult to disentangle even with My mercy.

You were predestined to reincarnate from your initial spiritual position to the world of suffering to serve humanity and thereby fulfill your divine duty. I have guided each of your steps to lead you back to the Tao. If you do not cooperate with each other in peace and harmony, I would be heartbroken watching you fall into the abyss.

You have to understand that and try to complete your tasks yourselves. If out of love, I had to do everything for you, and lead you by hand out of difficulties, you would not gain enough of your own merit and then have to reincarnate again many times before being able to return to your spiritual home.

Some of you became evil and fell into the seduction of the three-religions court. Be cautious on your way to complete your task. I would rather drop some of you in order to save the millions of humanity. Understand!

Tr., Your responsibility there is great, you should take care of the disciples.

Tr., do you know whom I trust among disciples?

Answer:...

Have any of you listened to My previous holy messages?

Except HTD., You are the disciple that I have ordered Saints and Immortals to guide, and you were close to Me during the spreading of the Tao. You have understood the way I used to found the Tao. Why were you so wrong in falling into evil seductions?

I don't use superstition. If you happened to be superstitious, did not follow the right way, and set up many nonsensical scenarios, the Tao would fall to heretics, as you may have seen.

Ascension.

October 27, 1927.

YOUR MASTER.

In antiquity, many martyrs were not as well blessed and recognized as you are now. What else are you expecting? You should not be discouraged.

The more one suffers and commiserates, the more one feels impatient. You should not feel regret, because suffering for millions of human beings is a worthy act.

As I have taught, just aspire to be able to love one another following My holy example. Love is the key to the thirty-six heavens, to Nirvana, and the White Jade Palace. Whoever denies love would never be able to escape reincarnation. And moreover, I will take care of all your difficulties, while I just ask for your love of each other and for your effort in serving humanity for its liberation.

Ascension.

Cholon, November 29, 1927

YOUR MASTER, children!

Tr.., I have many times counseled you disciples about using justice and concordance to fulfill your duty to the Tao; I am sad to see that you already have divisions among each other. You were concerned about your honor and secular advancement and forgot the worthy duties that I have entrusted to you. I have led you out of miserable situations, but you still have not put all your hearts together to prevent future difficulties; how would the Tao be established in time to save millions of human beings?

One is trying to build, ten others are trying to halt. You have ignored seniority among you and the divine titles that I have granted to you, and have used your power to oppress many gentle, virtuous disciples.

Alas! It has been but a few short days that you were separated from Me, and the great Tao has already become a worthless meeting! And the very ones who were disrupting the Tao are the torch bearers selected by the Three Religions Court to light the way for humanity. What would you think the future of the Tao would become? All my hard work of guiding you are just like drops of water in the waves of the ocean, and you are still drowning in the ocean of sufferings, far, far away from your original position. What a misery! What a regret!

I have said I set up evil beasts around you, but you did not heed my warning. How could I bend justice?

Many of you have neglected My words. Alas! Recalcitrant children! How can you avoid divine law? You have created aversion against the Three Religions Court, and therefore, it would be difficult for Me to save you. Although you have put your sincere heart into serving the Tao, it's still difficult to lift off all burdens. I would trust the Three Religions Court to decide on your destiny.

If any of you repents, the balance between the good and evil deeds may affect your chance.

Before I stopped the séances, I had clearly given orders as how to use spiritism. I thought you had announced My words to all dignitaries, so why the confusion? If you did not deliver My words, and they became confused, it is your responsibility.

Regarding female disciples, they seem as if they have never practiced the Tao; only one or two of them did, while hundreds of others were still just looking for entertainment. So, how could the Tao succeed? I said I trusted you to guide them; you must keep an eye on them in order to fix the problems in time to avoid big mistakes.

From now on, any time when you call for a meeting, you have to be present there yourself and follow My orders. There should be three responsible dignitaries of the Hiệp Thiên Đài to be present as witnesses, so that the decision of the meeting would be properly implemented.

N.., he lives too far away and will not be able to attend meetings regularly, while L… is still too much attached to secular business.

Alas! You have to withstand all the difficulties, especially at this moment. Tell C… to seriously heed My words. Arguments are merely profane, not able to shake the will of sincere disciples.

I bless you all.
Ascension.

Tayninh, the end of the year Đinh Mão (1927)

YOUR MASTER, children!

I have worked hard to guide you in the Tao, and you keep giving Me disappointment every day. I wonder when you would succeed! I have many times counseled you, and you did not take my counsels into account so that there are many difficulties right now.

Did you know that, if this were not the Third Universal Salvation, I would approve the Giáo Tông's recommendations to annihilate all your credits. But out of love, I counsel you again now so that you understand clearly the implementation of the Tao's policy.

You should understand that the Tao is based on love and sincerity. Love is to love living beings more than yourself, to consider them as important as Heaven and Earth, and consider yourself lightly. Sincerity is to deal with everything in secular and spiritual life with sincerity from the bottom of your heart. Even if you are extremely rich, if you don't have love and sincerity, you would never succeed in anything.

I recommend you to live according to the Tao, and not to try to render services to humanity just for honor or good reputation in this temporary world. You have to open your heart and your mind to practice the Tao, not thinking about being famous if the Tao succeeds. I shouldn't need to mention this, but I have to because many of you are still running after honor and position while practicing the Tao. If you have real sincerity for the Tao, there wouldn't be delay in the development of the Tao right now.

When I founded the Tao, I told you that you would be challenged by evil because you have not detached from secular attractions; otherwise, if you were strong enough to fight against evil, they would stay away, and the Holy See would be prosperous, and you all would be together as brothers and sisters in the same family, realizing heaven on earth. Wouldn't this be more worthy than being rich? Wouldn't this be the greatest blessing? Wouldn't this be the liberation for all humanity? Do you understand? It would be fortunate for the Tao if you do.

Let me ask you a question: what would the title and the position that I grant to you be good for? If you were detached from secular life and cling to the Tao, the Holy See wouldn't be insufficient in manpower and deteriorating. If you still want to serve the Tao, you should gather at the Holy See, and detach yourselves from secular matters. Take heed!

Ascension.

Year Mậu Thìn 1928

Nhàn Âm Đạo Trưởng

Dear disciples, if you want to cultivate your virtues, where should you start?

You should start right at your heart, which nobody can see. You cultivate your heart to perfection, then take care of outside appearance, and then you would have a solid physical and spiritual body that nobody can shake. If you keep paying attention to outside appearance and forgetting your heart, you are following the way of Hớn Lưu Bang dealing with his soldiers, which is like a person with only a physical body and no soul, or in other words, you pay attention to only visible matters and forget the miraculous mystic truth. Alas! One has a body with bone and skin but without a soul, which is useless like an inanimate boulder, or a plank of wood. It's like a lamp full of fuel but without a flame, not being able to light the darkness. Therefore, you have to cultivate the heart first, even if you do not see it, because if you don't cultivate the heart, and only pay attention to the outer appearance, it would be like reciting a prayer during a ceremony, with all physical lights shining, but without the Divine Eye illuminating your heart. Your ceremony would be empty, only paving the way to the emptiness of evil and falsehood.

Try to understand; otherwise, your work of cultivation would be useless.

Ascension.

February 3, 1928

YOUR MASTER.

Children! I am pleased to see changes in your practice and cooperation with each other on building the Tao. You should understand that any action in the Tao, if it pleases all dignitaries and disciples, would please Me.

As the Tao progresses every day, your road would be harder and harder to follow. But if you use your virtues instead of your power, your love toward others instead of the love of self, dedication toward the Tao instead of toward secular honors, you would be well on your way to reaching the goal of the Tao. Exactly like in secular life, in religious life if you are involved too much with your honors, powers, and position, you have to pay with difficulties, dangers, and suffering. You have to think about this and improve your virtues, being patient on your way, with perseverance to reach calmness in your conscience (heart). Those of you who are more interested in titles and powers will be at times punished. You should look at this as an example. You have heard My counsels regarding stopping spiritism, but many of you did not follow My orders and became lost on the wrong path. I shed tears in watching many beloved disciples falling into the abyss. Remember those examples and watch your step in the future.

I have shown you all possible options; you have to make up your mind and choose your way to go, with perseverance. It's a way to respect and love Me. Obey.

T..., T..., C..., from now on, you have to cooperate with each other to carry the load of the Tao. Anything that agrees with the New Codes pleases the divine will; anything consented to by all disciples, and useful for the Tao, should be implemented without waiting for My counsels.

When you trust, guide, and support each other without doubt and reservation, you have offered Me the greatest joy. For the traitor, the divine law will punish them accordingly.

C…, I forbid you to set up séances or automatic writings because they would cause great damage to the Tao. It would destroy the faith of humanity by leading them to impurity.

T…, I have mercy on you and excuse you. If you do it again, the Three Religions Court will excommunicate you. You should know that everyone has their own duty. If you don't fail, you would be in peace and joy. Try to heed My words.

I bless you all.

Ascension.

March 19, 1928

Here is THAI BACH

Great joy! Great joy!
Divine smile! I shall explain your titles. For example, if the title Thượng Đầu Sư, Ngọc Đầu Sư, Thái Đầu Sư, Hộ Pháp, Thượng Phẩm, Thượng Sanh, and even my tiltle Giáo Tông are granted to someone, this person would bear the title only but never become another Thái Bạch, another Thượng Trung Nhựt, or another Ngọc Lịch Nguyệt, or another Thái Nương Tinh, or another Hộ Pháp, or another Thượng Phẩm, or another Thượng Sanh.
Understand!
Ascension.

Holy See, the 10th day of the 3rd month of the year Mậu Thìn (1928)

YOUR MASTER, children!

C. H..., I see you bearing so much sadness and sufferings, I am joyful in shedding tears. (I don't understand) The secular road has many turning points with obstacles as arranged by divine will. It is a place for all Angels, Saints, Immortals and Buddhas to build their merit in order to return to their original positions. Humans are like merchants at a market, where all their strength, their mind, and their soul are worn down so that they have lost track of their soul, and their original positions.

Therefore, many Angels, Saints, Immortals, Buddhas have been contented with their lot, and did not dare to look up for any aspiration in order to avoid damnation. But if they dare not incarnate, they would be like students who avoid examinations; how could they regain their noble position? Life is like an examination; if it is easy to pass, the examination would not be valuable and meaningful. If the examination is difficult, and yet you pass the examination with honors, your success would be more valuable. In this world, you are the children I love most, but as an examiner, if I gave you the answers, your success at the examination would not be valuable.

Moreover, although I have never been away from you, I know that you are more than capable of passing the examination, and if I were to help you, I would damage the value of your honor.

The fact that you have to bear sufferings is from My will.

Being in a poor family yet having good virtues are good examples for other people. You should try to be patient, and your good virtues would be the ladder to heaven. The sincerity is for your cultivation, and the virtues are more precious than gold. Being contented with your poverty while you are practicing the Tao, your merits would be better than the ones of people of higher class.

Ascension.

April 2, 1928

YOUR MASTER, children!

I allow L... to come in. Children, you have to keep your promise to the Hiệp Thiên Đài. I have ordered Immortals to reveal to you some indispensable matters of the Tao, therefore, these current discontents in the Tao were already arranged and could not be prevented. You have to understand that each of you has your own great responsibility to the Tao. Before, when you took orders from the Three Religions Court to incarnate among human beings during this Third Universal Salvation, you had promised to fulfill your responsibility. I, as the Supreme Being who founded the Tao, also am obliged to guarantee your mission. Therefore, each of you has an important responsibility which, if you fail to fulfill, would lead to divine punishment according to the balance between your good and bad deeds. Satan has taken advantage of the crookedness of some of you, in order to compete with Me, to lure you to his side. He led disciples progressively according to their attitudes, away from the right path. As I had guaranteed your mission, and trained your holy mind, now is the time for the Three Religions Court to judge your actions according to justice.

Alas! Not too long in being away from Me, many of you were seduced by Satan because of your secular greed. I have pity for them, but I am unable to save them. Whoever follows the right path would have the opportunity to listen to My teachings. Whoever follows the wrong path would be led away by evil. If you happen to be able to distinguish between right and wrong, you should guide each other on My behalf and that of all living beings. Do not drop everything because you would have no way to fight against seductions; that would cause delay in the spreading of the Tao. You understand?

C..., T..., S..., You three have great responsibility to light the way at the beginning; I order you to cooperate with each other to build the Tao until the end.

Ascension.

April, 15 1928 (year Mậu Thìn)

YOUR MASTER, children!

(Laughter!) (Sigh!) My goodness! Look at you children! One is behaving this way, the other another way! Sad! Sad! Sad! T..., child! Many times, I have to suffer for taking care of you. My only wish is that you love each other in My holy virtue. I couldn't randomly and undeservedly give you all the supreme titles of Immortals and Buddhas. I have been bearing difficulties for you, only expecting you to love living beings and to spread the Tao. I have set up all means for you to have the wherewithal to establish the Tao successfully. I gave you the power to guide all souls who are suffering reincarnation. I have so decided and no one could change My decision.

Have you ever seen such an honor before? I gave each of you some power; I thought you should value it and improve your virtue a little, but many of you have disrespected Me, and did not listen to My orders to gather all My children into one family. Many people have complained. Under these circumstances, when would the Tao succeed?

Needless to say, whoever is a virtuous person, when they read the constitution of the Tao that I have created, should be very happy for humanity. I am obliged to promise to the Ngọc Hư Cung that if the Tao persists, I would remain with you and keep an eye on you. You see, My words are extremely important. If you value the Tao, you should put all your mind into following the constitution to organize the administration. The Hiệp Thiên Đài has not recognized you, and in the future, the Tao would not be recognized either. It is deserving of Me to correct this.

Though the Superior Spirits wanted the Tao to manifest strongly, I would not use spiritism to explain again, but rather leave all the responsibility in your hands. You should rely on yourselves to build up your own positions before humanity so that the Tao would appear as valuable as it should.

Therefore, I have to harness My heart to leave you alone although I have never been away from you. Do you understand?

Trust is given to teachers,
To mete discipline born of compassion.
Thusly influence humanity,
To build a world that evils must shun.

In you, as children, I have instilled virtue;
As adults you should strive to be virtuous!
Cleaving to your true spiritual selves,
Tho' this Earth be abject and tempestuous.

I bless you all.
T…, be patient and wait for My orders. You understand.
Ascension.

April 16, 1928
YOUR MASTER, Children!

As I have stated, I have treated all disciples as equals regardless of their titles. Whoever had built meritorious service in previous lives, I would trust them with more important responsibilities. Whoever had given less service I would give less responsibility. They all are my children. Except for administrative responsibilities, they are spiritually equal. No one can use their power to take advantage of others. Nobody has the right to abuse or disabuse anyone. Your purpose is the Tao; if you do not prize this goal, how could you avoid turmoil?

I am the Supreme Being. Many times in the past, I had to incarnate into the world to guide living beings. If I had not, there would not be all the religions that human beings are following today.

You must heed My teachings. There have been many Holy teachings from many Superior Spirits who, out of love, have guided you; however, you did not follow.

Ascension.

April 23, 1928

THANH TÂM

Greetings to all brothers
....

The Tao has been widely available; the seeds have been sown for two years, yet sincere followers are rare. This was the reason for the Gautama Sakya Muni Buddha's lamentation:

No people walk the street or plough the field.

No one is aware of the Tao; I fear for their destruction!

Do you understand, brothers?

Why did he say that there were no people walking the street, brother M...N...? There are lots of people in the street, but there are no *good* ones—there are only the walking dead, empty, deceitful, cruel people.

What did he mean by "nobody ploughs the field?" brother N. Đ...?

The heart is compared to the field. Nobody cultivates the *heart*, just as no one ploughs and prepares the field for growing rice. Fields left uncultivated become the province of snakes, rats, insects. People with fallow, uncultivated hearts become like vermin.

The field is ready; so are the seeds and the implements. People just need to take up the plough and do the necessary work to bring in the harvest. If they don't plough—in other words, cultivate the heart—then they shall not reap. They'll lose their soul! The last verse reflects this result.

Ascension.

Tây Ninh Holy See, the 5th day of the 5th month of the year Mậu Thìn (6-22-1928)

YOUR MASTER!

Children, each of you have chosen your own path. I am grieved by the disagreement among. I shall leave you alone to decide how to be: virtuous or evil. If you are of a determined and strong character, the Tao would be in harmony, and you shall advance toward My presence; if you vacillate in your virtue, the road of notoriety shall lead you to the abyss. Expending your strength on dividing yourselves would simply exhaust you; you would have nothing left over to uplift, support or counsel one another.

The fair and just path that can save living beings is the path of the Tao. The divine light is always illuminating that path for you. It's totally averse to Evil. Remember My words. Do not neglect them, but instead contemplate them carefully in order to understand.

What a disaster! Many times you did not heed My words, and I was heartbroken to see you get lost. Alas, such challenges must be put to profane minds!

Ascension.

Holy See, the 11th day of the 5th month of the year Mậu Thân (6/28/1928)

YOUR MASTER, Children

H..., let me tell you how to refine sugar. Do you know how to make black sugar into white?
(H...H... Master, I don't know).
Listen.
Pour black sugar into a jar with a hole in the bottom until two-thirds full. Then fill the jar with mud to the rim. Expose the jar to the sun for one week. When you remove the mud, you will have sugar all sparkly white and delicious.
Your sufferings are like this sugar*, My child. Do you know that I have wept as you do?
If I had not, how could you be My child? Just remember that I love you; that would be enough. You should not trade the love of the world for My discontentment; rather you should suffer the hate of the world but deserve instead My love. What would you gain if you meet with My discontentment?
C..., CH Take care of the meditation hall along with your younger brothers.
T..., you have become lazy!
C..., call your two older brothers to attend the great corbeille à bec. Don't let them continue to be skeptical!
Ascension.

*Comment from the translator: the heart exposed to sufferings would be purified like the sugar under the mud.

The 4th day of the 6th month of the year Mậu Thân (1928)

You are a ship aware of its own destiny,
A soul tossed on tempest's wave.
It's time to pray for God's mercy,
As one who recalls the blessings He gave.

Tiêu Sơn Taoist

The Tao has just passed through many difficulties; however, it is still endangered. Be cautious of your steps so that your efforts are not wasted.

Know yourself, know the Tao. Know the situation, know the people; know the difference between good and evil, right and wrong, in order to adjust your actions.

The Tao is not yet manifest because people still lack virtue. Virtuous people lack clear vision. Intelligent people lack godliness, modesty, sincerity. People on the whole still yearn for wealth and honor.

Bustling upon the same road, pushing toward the same destination, most fail to yield to one another. Those who are downtrodden are accosted by others sure of their bearings; others rush forward without heeding pitfalls. In this situation, nobody wins, no one is wiser, and the road to Glory is deserted. Persons of evil hearts and stained souls are incapable of guiding others on the right path. Do not count on the notorious as exemplars; better to take account of yourself.

The followers of the Tao have witnessed dignitaries engendering separation; this is the fruit of evil minds. The Hiệp Thiên Đài, a miraculous and precious organization, has become useless because of the errors of some dignitaries. No wonder the Tao is in turmoil! The Hiệp Thiên Đài is supposed to be the foundation supporting the Tao but is no longer trustworthy, dooming the Tao for the foreseeable future. The world has become a nonsensical realm where might makes right. Be careful!

The Hiệp Thiên Đài is headed by the Supreme Being, Who bears supreme judgment over all. The New Code is still deficient because dignitaries from the Hiệp Thiên Đài do not themselves heed it. This chaotic situation has resulted in the power of the Cửu Trùng Đài. You will receive more instructions later. Many parts need clarification.

If you followers know your limits and keep yourselves from defaming the Tao, you will hold its miraculous key in the future.

Transgressions will receive judgment; good works will be rewarded. Try to maintain your position. Try to understand Me.

Ascension.

7/18/1928

Chơn Cực Lão Sư (Taoist Master)

Greetings to followers:

You have listened to Holy Teachings regarding the destiny of the Tao. Have you understood the forthright goal of the Tao? M.N., try to tell me.

It's the administration. How about the goal? What is cooperation for? What is brotherly love for? You understand, but not profoundly.

You should know that before spreading the Tao to foreign countries, you have to develop a secure connection with people of this Southern country, to guide them out of this suffering world and create a peaceful life. At that time, just like birds returning to their nests, and fish to the streams, people will climb back upon the spiritual ladder.

As long as there is no concordance in the Tao, people strive to control each other rather than show the way with a clear, impassioned mind; the disciples remain greedy and base-willed, attracted by honors and wealth. The Tao cannot succeed under such circumstances, and none of you may find the way home to your divine position. You disciples need to be selective in your choices to find people with sincerity and determination to cooperate in building a common house, so that sometime in the future you may enjoy the prosperity of the Tao, rather than still subsisting on the physical plane, frantic in mind and spirit all day with no time to think about the future of your souls.

The Tao is not a funeral home nor a market; nothing is for sale here as you may have thought.

What a sadness! Some followers are as ungainly as a newlywed stumbling blindly into the bridal chamber for the first time, both mind and feet numb. Some untalented souls still battle with and denigrate each other, only proving themselves inferior.

Out of love, the Supreme Being has sown seeds of the Tao, to bring the lifeboat ashore for all people to sail to Nirvana. But how can one who cannot comprehend escape drowning? The Tao deteriorates with the separation between people; though gathered from many disparate places, you must finally reconcile the disparities between yourselves.

M... N... Use rituals as instructed at the Cầu Kho's séance. Do not invent new ones

(Văn Pháp addressed....)

Indeed, but there is still insufficiency. You need to abandon anything that is not useful save the music and the solemnity of the rituals.

There is still deficiency in the music as well. The music for greeting Superior Spirits should be different; musicians should dress cleanly and purely, and musical pieces should be played in clear harmonies. You should improve it.

You should not attend any temples where the rituals differ from these instructions.

Ascension.

Cholon, July 28, 1928 (year Mậu Thìn)

YOUR MASTER, children

You have been without My holy teachings for quite a while now. I felt your desire for Me to come back to guide you. I am sad to see you children foundering in this mundane existence.

Children, out of love, I guide you like a father raising a child, watching them grow, expecting them to mature into a great person, leaving their name to future generations. The manifestation of the Tao greatly moves My authority, My honor, even My position. I am glad in your success, sad in your failure, and I suffer when you suffer. In this world, both contentment and repentance are like rivers and mountains that I created. They may merge, rivers into rice fields, mountains into valleys and oceans, sadness into elation, fame into ignominy and scorn, peace into disasters.

I have mercy for those of you who dare to denounce your secular life, to follow Me to guide your incredulous younger brothers and sisters. But alas, how cruel mortality! A lowly insect may ruin a golden harvest; the men at the helm of karma can founder even the Heavenly Lifeboat. I hope you may understand.

Children, the more I am moved by your sincerity, your impartiality, and your modesty, the more I would like to erase all cunning and treacherous people, who are always running after honors and wealth, from the Earth.

Alas! I have belabored myself over your plight, hoping each of you would be awakened, realize you have strayed, and step off your interminable paths to return to the right path and follow Me once more. That would please Me most.

Tr..., Don't fret! I have pre-arranged an appropriate position for each of you. The disaster will soon be over. Take comfort and be at peace so that I can rely upon you. Understand My divine authority is reserved to guide all of you, not for its own sake. Be of noble mind in order to bear the hardships which befall all beings.

Secular life is mundane and rife with temporal attractions, but the Tao is eternal.

Weigh the true importance of matters taking place in the illusory world; trust in Me. I have arranged your life and your destiny.

Tr..., you understand?

Tr..., try to console your spouse, and follow Lý Bạch's words. Those are two matters that I entrust to you.

Blessings to you all.

Ascension.

Cầu Nhiếm, the 19th of the 6th month of the year Mậu Thìn (August 5, 1928)

YOUR MASTER, children

Tr…, Th…! You two have dedicated your time to travel to spread the Tao, yet you don't comprehend the current situation of the Tao. The Tao presently is an undiagnosed patient at the threshold of malignancy; without treatment, the malady expands from within, unrecognized, with deadly power over the life of the patient.

You might think the Tao has prospered, but there is internal poverty. Consider the Sở dynasty trying to control the Tan dynasty; in the Sở dynasty, people are divided behind an aura of external strength. If this division is not rectified, the Sở dynasty will fall. Everyone likes to enjoy personal sovereignty. No different for spokesmen of the Tao, but they become like merchants battling merchants for ownership of the goods! What is the reason for such a farce? They lack self-regulatory skills, are arrogant and thirsty for high titles and honors, and do not possess the necessary virtues to administer people, thus creating animosity. You two should realize this weakness and find ways to create harmony and cooperation between disciples so that they would look to the Holy See and pray for blessings. Each of you has the responsibility to cease your own hatred, correct your attitudes, rally educated persons to the cause, and lead people to recognize the pricelessness of the Tao.

In time, vacillation will yield to surety, the few to the millions, and the guidance of disciples will hold sway in the face of obstacles.

One day of delay in the spreading of the Tao means one day of harm to the people. If each of you keeps causing animosity among people, the Tao would become a farce, and when would there be completion? When would the Tao be spread across the Earth?

If you still harbor confusion within, how can you create harmony without? You are well aware that since antiquity, anything going against people's hearts would not last. The practice of cooperation in peace should be the only practice to be applied to the Tao.

The arrogant want only to be served; they care not for the humble or modest among society. Such are the kings who destroy their own kingdoms. Organizing a congregation is not much different from organizing a country; in fact, your duty and responsibility are greater and more difficult. You must correct yourself, and reconcile with others so as to prevent the destruction of the Tao. Create harmony, cooperation, solidarity and freedom among people. This would be the most precious achievement ever.

Out of love for living beings and empathy for all your striving, I have no heart to let the congregation deteriorate, but if among you, no one takes the responsibility to create harmony, then animosity between people would cause chaos, ruining My efforts of guiding you since the beginning. Then would you drown in the ocean of suffering evermore. If you won't love one another, then the more numerous, only the more turmoil, animosity, and disparities you would create, until you all become totally useless. Understand!

I bless you all.

Ascension.

The Year of the Earth Dragon (1928)

Children, your Master proclaims:
DO NOT KILL LIVING BEINGS!

I have told you that when there was nothing in this universe, the cosmic ether gave birth only to Me, and My throne is the universal monad. I divided the monad into the diad which is Yin and Yang, and then into the tetrad and then into the eight trigrams. The latter changes continuously to form the universe. I then divided My spirit to create ten thousand things, from elements to finally living beings: plants, insects, animals and humans.

You should understand that everything emanates out of My spirit; wherever there is life, there am I. I am the progenitor of life. My love of life is unfathomable. Life is given freely to all living beings out of My Being. I distribute life everywhere in the universe. Life erupts like a flower from a tree: it develops from the bud into bloom, and evolves to form fruit that seeds more trees ad finitum. If someone cuts that flower, the fruit of life is interrupted and future evolution is prevented.

Each life has its own Karmic plan. It does not matter whether it is an original or secondary living being,* its life on this earth is divinely appointed. If you kill any living being, you shall be punished; no one knows whether a living being may have been an Immortal or a Buddha reincarnating to Earth. As I have said, all life is Me. To destroy life is to attempt to destroy Me. And it is not easy to destroy Me. Teach that to human beings.

Ascension.

---

* *Original living being: a living being whose spirit is directly coming from God's spirit.*
Secondary living being: a living being whose spirit is coming from the original living being. The original living being may divide his/her spirit to form many living beings, who are called secondary living beings.

The Year of the Earth Dragon (1928)

Children, your Master proclaims:
DO NOT STEAL.

Alas! When I created you, I loved and respected you so profoundly, I sent you to this world with a sacred body made in My own image, so that originally you did not need to eat in order to live, or to make clothes to cover yourself.

However, you did not listen to Me but were seduced by materials, tastes, sexuality, power and wealth, which ultimately led to suffering in this world. I reserved enough wealth for all of you to share, but because of greed, some of you took too much, leaving others to suffer hunger without sustenance.

I granted the same powers to you that I granted to the Genies, Saints, Immortals, and Buddhas so that you could discipline yourselves to respect and honor My saintly love of life. Unfortunately, these powers have become a tool to treat other beings as slaves. Alas! What a tragedy! I am so disappointed! Do you know why people become so dishonest and greedy?

The principal needs of people are food and clothing--no one can avoid those needs. Unfortunately, many people bicker for exclusivity over the distribution of these necessities, and put their own needs above others'. They struggle for material goods beyond all reason, stockpiling beyond all possible need, regaling in trickery and evil to satisfy their cravings for material gain. And how do they acquire this power? They bend the meek to their will until the power is betrothed to them to call evil, good. The brutes acquire all, while the meek loses all. Thus society falls into chaos. There is no justice as God's laws are no longer observed; this is the cause of all suffering on Earth.

When dishonesty and greed penetrate your heart, there is no room for virtue. When they penetrate your home, there can be no moral teachings.

When they penetrate your country, there can be no honorable administration. When they penetrate the world, Genies and Saints cannot arise.

Crime is the natural outcome of dishonesty and greed; therefore, dishonesty and greed in the heart, even unmanifest, are crimes against God's laws.

Ascension.

Year of the Earth Dragon (1928)

Children, your Master proclaims:

DO NOT BE OBSCENE.
Why is obscenity a severe crime?

Ordinary people see the physical body as a single unit. In reality, it is a mass of innumerable living cells, assembled to form a body with a divine essence. This body is nourished by living beings such as vegetable matter, fruit, and rice; these all contain vital matter, as all these foods are fresh with the essence of life and potential, they are not dead. Foods already dead do not carry this life essence and potential. Cooking by steam or quick-frying simply disinfects foods and prepares them for our digestion. The nutritional energy of these foods does not disintegrate after being cooked.* Foods are then transformed in your gastrointestinal system into "Khí" (vital energy), and then their life essence is carried into the blood. As you have been taught, there is spiritual energy in "Khí" and in blood. It is transmuted from spirit into the human body as a result of the cycle of [death and] birth. Therefore, even a drop of blood has contained a certain amount of spiritual energy.

Since sexual "Tinh" life matter is composed partly of blood and partly of "Khí," excessive sexual activity thus causes an unnecessary expenditure of Tinh and therefore of spiritual energy. After your death, you will be confronted with and judged by this spiritual energy about the way you wasted it, at the "Nghiệt Cảnh Đài."** You will not be able to deny how you wasted your spirit. So, you should observe this precept closely.

Ascension.

---

* *Foods change only in form during the process of digestion and absorption. Foods do not die after being cooked or digested because they constitute elements comprised of atoms. Atoms are not destroyed--they only change their arrangement, form and purpose.*

** *"Nghiệt Cảnh Đài" is a place in the spiritual world where the spirits, after the death of their physical body, will revisit all their actions—both good and bad—they have committed during their physical lifetime.*

January 18, 1927. Year of the Fire Tiger.

DO NOT DRINK ALCOHOL.

(DO NOT INTOXICATE YOURSELF.)

Why abstain from intoxication?

I have taught that your body is composed of a mass of everlasting spirits contained within living units. You should understand that the internal organs of your body are also formed by these living units whose function, whether they are aware of it or not, is commanded by Me. I therefore use your body to teach.

Firstly, I'll explain why alcohol is harmful to your physical body. Your physical body is still like an animal's and needs to eat in order to live. When alcohol is ingested, it is absorbed into all internal organs of your body including the heart which is the foremost mechanism of life. Alcohol forces the whole cardiovascular system to function excessively, and the lungs do not have adequate time to purify (oxygenate and purge carbon dioxide) the blood, so that waste products will accumulate in the whole body, polluting the living units, leading to progressive sickness and finally to the demise of the living units of the organs and then of your whole body. Many people's bodies are half-dead just because of alcohol.

Secondly, I'll explain why alcohol is harmful to your spirit.

I have said that the soul forms the "second body." It is composed of the "Khí," which surrounds your body like a mold. Its center is the brain, and the portal by which your second body enters and exits is the fontanelle on top of the head which is guarded by the Hộ Pháp. (With meditation, there is unification of the "Tinh," the "Khí" and the "Thần," leading to enlightenment).

The brain is thus the origin of the "Khí." When polluted blood accumulates in the brain, the brain is disrupted by confusion and languor so that your spirit and human intelligence are clouded, no longer in control of the body. The body will lose its human personality and revert to its animal essence. Lost is the hope to advance to the states of Genie, Saint, Immortal, and Buddha. At the same time, when the brain is confused, it becomes an open gate for evil, wreaking havoc on your environment and pushing your soul into continuous reincarnation. Therefore, listen, I forbid you to drink alcohol!

Ascension

Year of the Earth Dragon (1928)

Children, your Master proclaims:
DO NOT SIN BY WORD.

Why is lying forbidden?
I have said that I have set up a spirit in your physical body that protects your life. As you have been taught, this spirit is impartial and can communicate with the Genies, Saints, Immortals, Buddhas, and Superior Spirits of the Ngọc Hư Cung (Cabinet of God) and can record all of your good and bad actions. They then transmit this (Akashic) record to the Celestial Judgment Court. All will be recorded there.

Moreover, this holy spirit not only has a duty to protect you, but to educate you as well, through what most people describe as the "conscience." Thus, Confucian Saints have said: "One who despises people despises one's own heart. God has determined that this is a crime from which there is no escape." When you lie to people, you first lie to yourself, to your own conscience, and thus to your own spirit (which is a part of God).

As I have said, this spirit will submit your every word to the Celestial Judgment Court--and even though you may never have acted on your words, you will be punished for them just the same, because the effect on the spirit (and therefore on God) will have been the same. Therefore, at the Celestial Judgment Court, none of your words will be omitted. This is why I have instructed you to be careful in your words and your virtues. You should be twice as careful in your speech as in your actions, because the punishment for morally reprehensible speech is the same as punishment for morally reprehensible actions.

It would be wise for you to remember this.
Ascension.

Year Kỷ Tỵ (February 10, 1929)

YOUR MASTER, children

Time is creeping by, yet the road to the Tao seems endless. Each year, you have to walk a mile, but in looking at you disciples, I find you still hesitating to take a step forward. Alas! Time inexorably flows, and while your self-cultivation of virtue is stalled, your tendency to stray off the path is not! You would let the great spiritual foundation I have set out for you all go to ruin, as you compete to be the worst of the worst, leading to deep division among the congregation. Brutish people are still entranced by honors and wealth; there would seem to be no way to cure this disease infecting the Tao. I am so heartbroken, but I Myself will not change you. I have entrusted important responsibilities to the most reliable among you, but they were too disillusioned to manage these responsibilities, and the congregation was invaded by evildoers.

Alas! Time has flown away; so has your life and the life of the Universe. Children! If you could only bear the difficult situations of life, concede honors, sacrifice self for others, shed tears in exchange for the joy of others, sustain hardship in your livelihood, keep your mind clean and clear, to be touched by others' sufferings, your soul would be purified, and you would be able to return to Me.

You should correct yourself without delay. Try to cooperate with each other to shun the evildoers; this would sustain your merit.

I bless you all.

Ascension.

Tây Ninh Holy See, April 16, 1929 (the 7th day of the 3rd month, midnight)

YOUR MASTER, children

M… Ng…, ask your brothers to call the female disciples up here, the poor women kneeling down there!

I told you clearly that Thượng Phẩm had to return to Me before all of you, but out of sloth, you did not read My holy teachings in order to know.

T…! Do you remember I told you that the Tao is the nothingness; if Thượng Phẩm does not return to his divine position, who is going to guide souls to the celestial gate? Moreover, you are guiding living beings in this world on My behalf; so, there should be someone on the divine plane to receive those souls. (Smiling!)

Th…! You have to build a tomb for Thượng Phẩm in front of the tree with three branches, facing East, like facing Me at the altar. The roof should be of three levels, and covered with tiles exactly like the roof of a Chinese pagoda. Don't build it like Bảo Đạo's tomb, because their titles are different. Around its base, the octagonal tomb should look like it has posts. There should be a hole at the top center to allow the sunlight to shine upon the coffin.

You will be reprimanded by Thái Bạch. Try to follow his counsels to correct yourselves and make peace with him.

Heed Me!

Ascension.

January 11th, 1930 (the 12th day of the 12th month of the year Kỷ Tỵ)

YOUR MASTER, children

I've often told you that you are the body of love, and you don't even know what it is, where it is from? T..., try to find out.

(T... responded)

No, child! Love is the source of life in the universe.
With love, all living beings can be at peace and the universe tranquil. With peace and tranquility, there would be no animosity, no mutual destruction, and subsequently there would be maintenance of life and evolvement.

Do you know who is against life and evolvement? T..., try to find out!

(T... responded)

No! You are blaming evil spirits, but in reality, Satan is the one who destroys evolvement. I am life and Satan death. Tell Me how Satan can harm you.

(T... responded: Satan induces people into hatred to create turmoil among people).

Why don't you use the word "death" to express it more profoundly? Because of hatred, people would despise, then fight each other, leading to the destruction of the world. Therefore, from now on, if you cannot love each other, I forbid you to hate each other. Obey!

Ascension.

Tây Ninh, February 7th, 1930 (the 9th day of the 1st month of the year Canh Ngọ)

YOUR MASTER.

Children, I am determined to manifest Tao out of Love, to save humanity in this last era. But the congregation is not perfected; the path has not reached its goal. Many of you have not had good faith in listening to Holy Teachings, thus the congregation is shattered.

Virtuous people became sad and discouraged, and sincere people are not happy to participate. Evildoers have invaded the congregation; wicked, ill-minded people, leading to the deterioration of the cultivation of love and virtue, straight to the wrong path.

The Tao is invaluable and miraculous. When one understands the Tao, one knows self, knows people, knows the situation, knows the moment, understands the non-permanency of honors, distinguishes persistence from death, develops a conscience. One would know that life is a farce full of suffering for its human actors. The wise man distinguishes honorable actions from shameful ones, and thus knows how to manage one's life. He overcomes the present kind of infighting and competition, through which there would be no hope of reaching immortality or Nirvana.

My blessings were shattered by greedy and ignorant disciples, under the influence of greed for honors and wealth. With the perpetration of these evils, they have led humanity into the abyss, rather than to the Tao; thus has the spirit of the Tao become faint for thousands of years.

Many of you have tried to sacrifice self to become leaders of the Tao. But have any of you yet deserved the title? M... Ng ?

M... Ng... answered: ....

Alas! For the sake of millions of souls, I wouldn't have the heart to see all your positions destroyed. Based strictly upon divine justice, none of you deserve to succeed. The practice of the Tao is the opposite of living the secular life. It must be that way in order overcome the mundane and get closer to the divine illumination. I have noticed that many of you on one hand want to practice the Tao, but on the other hand don't want to abandon secular life; the secular life would extinguish the divine flame. You have to have a very strong mind to resist the secular path, or all your efforts toward illuminating the Tao would be in vain.

You want to wear religious raiment and stand in front of human beings as religious leaders, ostensibly to follow the paths of Saints and Immortals. But at the same time, you are still seduced by wealth and influence, using the name of the Tao to build up your own name. You build mansions on earth, wear suits of silk with gold-lined pockets—of what are you the Master? Better to be master of your soul, clothed in virtue, building your mansion in heaven! Alas! Alas! What religious garb you do wear! Wayward children who resist my teachings!

In ancient times, followers of the Tao survived dire sufferings, living by self-sacrifice and enduring abject poverty for their souls' sake, never seduced by honors and wealth. They earned divine positions. They were not like those of you today who prefer wealth to empathy, power to virtue, division to brotherhood. You are averse to sacrifice yet contend to be following the right path. Now I ask you, whosoever would agree?

Your music and rituals are not worthy. You are putting on such airs of superiority, relying on others' talent and claiming it as your own; it doesn't take Confucius to quote Confucian books! You will be tried under divine jurisprudence for your impudence. Whoever realizes his divine origin, and repents his worldly flaws, escapes divine wrath and evil pitfalls on his way to the Tao. But what a shame that this congregation has sunk so low! Now you must take on the responsibility with which I've entrusted you, to cooperate with one another in the salvation of living beings for eternity.

M…N…, I allow you to show My holy teachings to your brothers Tr…, Tr…. If the rituals at the Holy See are not perfected as I have previously instructed, evil would come and take control.

I counsel you:
With sincerity, follow the steps of the Tao,
Renounce riches and secular honor,
Bear up under sackcloth and poverty,
That you may avoid the clutches of Karma.
I bless all of you.

Ascension.

April 12, 1930 (the 17th day of the 3rd month of the year Canh Ngọ)

Nhàn Âm Đạo Trưởng (Nhàn Âm Taoist Master)

Greetings to all disciples.

It has been a long time since I have addressed you about the Tao. Today, I'd like to congratulate some of you, who have put all your mind and heart into self-cultivation, but I am sad for many others, who value secular life more than the progress of your soul. The Supreme Being has forgiven you out of love, hoping for peace in the congregation someday. Therefore, you have to cooperate with one another and get back to guiding people in the Tao. This is the only way to repent, and to improve yourselves in order to return to your original spiritual positions. You should have concern for your own futures.

H...., are you now more learned in Vietnamese literature? Many followers have deeply studied the Holy Teachings, so I would ask you to interpret the following poem:

On the way Home, never mind stumbling blocks,
Slowly but surely, you would reach Nirvana.
(1) Though the stomach is empty, the crane is free.
(2) Though fully fed, the rooster is caged.
(3) Behold all the abandoned tombs of youth,
(4) And the surface of water always rippled by the wind.
Each turn of life leads up one step,
If you hesitate, time evaporates.

(Many people interpreted the poem but without understanding of the four central verses, so explanation is given:)

Verses (1) and (2) are from the poem of Lý Bạch:

The rooster in the cage, although being fully fed every day, would not know when it is going to be slaughtered,

While the crane, although not having enough to eat, is able to fly freely in the sky.

In other words, one would rather be suffering and free, than comfortable yet doomed. Being one with the Tao, one would be divinely free like the crane, although suffering in the physical plane.

Explanation of the verses (3) and (4):
If one looked into who were buried in those abandoned tombs, one would find that they all died young. Life is like a brief ripple in water; one may die at any time. If one does not hasten to follow the Tao, one may die before finding It.

Sakya Muni Buddha has said:
Don't wait until becoming old to learn the Tao,
For many are the abandoned tombs of youth.
You disciples understand?

Verse (4): The water's surface rippled by the wind, is like a human face grimacing under the weight of the mortal coil; only the Tao can help one escape this oppression.

Old literature has also said:
The mountaintop is white, not from great age but from the snow,
The lake ripples, not from angst but from the winds that blow.
Try to understand.
Every body understands the last two verses.
You disciples try to learn the Tao. Obey!

Ascension.

The 23rd day of the 3rd month of the year Canh Ngọ (4-21-1930)

Re-evocation.
YOUR MASTER, children

Tr..., because of love, I founded the Tao according to the divine mechanism to guide millions of souls to return to their original position. I know that many souls have re-incarnated with a mission of guiding humanity. They did not mind hard work. So I have asked the three religions court to be clement to them so that they may save you.

Alas! Superior Spirits and I have been working hard to help, but you didn't have much sincerity. Many times Superior Spirits wanted to drown all of you, but I was so heart broken, so worried, and shedding tears that I have modified the divine mechanism to let you have more time, more strength, to guide each other to fulfill your duties. However, evils still prevailed. Secular seductions have led you to the wrong path. I am heart broken to watch you lost in evil way. Some of you were attracted by money, others by lust, others by power and wealth, others ended up committing crimes. All of them by their own way have lost their divine mind, wandering along evil caverns.

Even worse, evils were mingling among you creating separation between you, severing your co-operation, your connection, stimulating you to fight against each other so that you became weakened, having no more strength to resist. Finally, you were badly broken in pieces and fell into abyss.

I thought I would leave you alone to compete with each other and to fight against evils, but in looking at the divine book, 80% of you would fall into evil hands. Most of you were high spirits with important responsibility, I felt obliged to bend the justice, and reveal to you some secrets that might help you to correct your own steps, to cure each others' diseases, and to prevent future similar occurrence.

Evils have prevailed. How could you resist? You were the ones that I trusted at the beginning, although you have made wrong steps on many occasions, but thanks to the merciful guidance of Superior Spirits, you have corrected yourselves on time. I have pity for many others, who fell in evil hands, and became drown forever, without even tasting the pleasure of power, wealth, or lust.

The Tao is powerful, but evil power is not negligible. If you could not control your temper, the fire inside your heart would be induced by evils to burn yourselves. Try to understand My words. If you don't use the authority that I granted to you to guide your younger brothers to fight against evils, the latter will lure them all away later on. You are then the only one left, like a single bird, or a lost phoenix, you would have no more energy to get out of the storm. At that time, the world would change, you would be exiled to the 72nd planet, the lowest planet with more sufferings. Realize your important responsibility. If you could not make it, you could not return to your original position at the end of the divine path.

B...! I have blessed you. You deserve My holy blessings, which would protect you. Why didn't you fulfill your important responsibility? Why did you hurt others? The chief of Pnom Penh congregation has taken My order to guide people. The more important is the responsibility, the more difficult is the performance. If you don't have enough patience and hurt him, he may resign like Lý Bạch did previously, you would have no hope to accomplish your journey.

I am heart broken to watch the divine book. Those are the last important words for you. It's the same thing right here as well as in Pnom Penh. You should co-operate with each other to disentangle the difficulty. Obey!

I bless all of you.

Ascension.

The 12th day of the 5th month of the year Canh Ngọ (June 8, 1930)

Here is Quan Thánh Đế Quân (Kwan Kung)

Greetings to all disciples,

The congregation has not yet been established, but people are already lazy to cultivate their holy virtues, and want even to compare themselves to Superior Spirits, in trying to show off their broad knowledge.

The situation of the world has changed. According to the divine book, the global disasters are very close. From the South to the North, from the East to the West, chaos has risen occasionally destroying cruel people. Even with divine spirit inside, if aren't awakened, people would be destroyed. Alas! The divine light has shined people's mind, but they are still confused and tried to use their little mind to fight against the creator. They wished to follow the Tao, but if they kept bargaining, it's difficult for the Mercy Father to please them, no matter what their title is.

Shouldn't they follow the example of ancient Superior Spirits, who had endured a lot of sufferings, and achieved great services to humanity in order to return to their noble position?

In this illusory life, your existence is like water bubbles or floating clouds. You should repent, return to the right path, cultivate your good virtues, you may have a chance to avoid the trap of evils. Arrogance is the grave to bury yourself. Remember that in order to correct yourself. Try to contemplate on the following poem:

World's examples are not good enough lessons to make you perfect,
Growing old, but still confused between fame and shame.
Possessing pearls, you would have difficulty to cultivate your holy virtues,
In front of gold, you would be unable to enforce discipline.
Already divinely blessed, but you are still trying to bargain,

And even to fight against each other for the wealth that you haven't seen.

World's situation keeps evolve, and disasters start to rise,

That you should realize before going forward to compete with each other.

You divinely appointed disciples should explain this poem to living beings.
Ascension.

The 12th day of the 5th month of the year Canh Ngọ (June 8, 1930)

Here is Nhàn Âm Đạo Trưởng,

Greetings to brothers and sisters,

I follow the order of the Supreme Being to address to my beloved brothers and sisters.

I am sad for human beings, who haven't had the chance to follow the Tao, so that they are drown in the suffering ocean, when the judgment day arrives. It's difficult to save them. Natural disasters happen, and it's heart breaking to see human beings floundered in the suffering ocean, while the saving boat is also struck by huge breaker and unable to save people.

The Tao stands majestically in Vietnam to protect the blessed people. However, if they are not awakened, continue to be hesitating in the firm and strict self cultivation, they would not be able to avoid destruction.

I recommend you to look up to the Supreme Being with all your sincerity in order to receive blessings leading you to the free and happy path. You may have some petty difficulties in your family, but if you compare that to the extreme love of life of the Supreme Being, the bright virtuous path would surely lead you one step closer to the extreme ecstasy.

When you are with the Tao, you may have to sacrifice your personal secular life in order to fulfill your responsibility of saving millions of people.

You would not regret for your sacrifice and sufferings. That is the attitude of the Saint who practices the true Tao. Remember.

Ascension.

The 5th day of the 5th month of the year Canh Ngọ (June 10, 1930)

Here is LY BACH

Greetings to all friends.
....
The Tao is not a merchandise that you have to beg people to buy or to recognize. It would be a shame for the Tao.

The Supreme Being has already sown the precious seeds, your responsibility is to care for the plant. If the plant grows strong, blooms with beautiful flowers, it would bear precious fruits. At that time, people from thousands of miles far away, would follow the fragrance to come ask for the precious fruits. You would not need to put yourself down to beg people.

You disciples keep following straight your way, co-operate with each other to achieve your own duty, everything would be successful as arranged by the Supreme Being.

Friend Tr..., you understand clearly? You have seriously mistaken. You have sold the fame of the Tao once, you should try to claim it back. The Holy See is the origin, once it stands majestically at this area, people would beg you to allow them to join. Try to understand to take care of it.

....
Ascension.

Holy See, December 24th, 1930 (year Canh Ngọ)
Đại Đạo Tam Kỳ Phổ Độ
Here is Lý Giáo Tông

Greetings to all friends and young sisters.

I have great affection for you. I have been out of secular life for a long time so that I feel a little strange in evaluating people's mind. Alas! What a difficulty! Because earlier, I saw such a big crowd of children of the Supreme Being in this little country Vietnam, I could not imagine the crowd once the Tao is spread to all over the five continents.

I am tired of this great responsibility! Because of my promise to the Great Mercy, and of my duty as an elder brother, I have to use my power to discipline you, although I have understood your mind. The only thing that I am afraid of is that I could not get closer to evil people to teach them. It's easier to get close to virtuous people, but it's not necessary, because they all have holy hearts, which are genuinely beautiful in any suffering situation of the world, and which would secure them their divine position without help from anybody. Therefore, what I need to do is to sow the holy seeds into the heart of evil people, hoping for a change, but not to worry about saving virtuous people.

Like you, my duty is to change the world. We would be more comfortable if we know our capability. We have to adjust ourselves according to the situation. Difficult situations would produce talented people. If there are obstacles, there would be favorable times. We need to be patient to observe all aspects of life.

Dear friends and sisters, you have witnessed many hardships and sufferings during the year of the opening of the congregation. I am well aware of that and could not have the heart to watch. I am determined to stand next to you, shoulder to shoulder to share all miserable times.

It's not that I am afraid for me, because no power of this visible world could touch me. I am just afraid for you, who bear a physical body, and therefore could not stand all oppression. You friends and sisters don't have the power of prediction in order to avoid those situations.

So thought, I am determined to take back my authority, using my divine eyes to recognize the situations for you, in order to win the battle against evils at this time. I think I wouldn't be useless.

I have a close affection with a spiritual friend, who had volunteered to incarnate to the world to save living beings, and then had sustained many sufferings. I have to say that the reward and punishment mechanism of the divine book is beyond human imagination. Many times the worldly rewards are the spiritual punishments, and vice versa. Therefore, although you could not understand, you should be cautious about the punishments and the rewards that I implement in the congregation administration. You should not argue foolishly, criticize blindly, and then waste your life by committing spiritual crimes. Obey!

Ascension.

The 9th day of the 2nd month of the year Tân Mùi (4-26-1931)

JADE EMPEROR ALIAS CAO ĐÀI

Greetings to all disciples,

Tr..., the congregation is tumbled down because of the divine arrangement. The country is at times in peace, at times in turmoil, life is at times prosperous, at times deteriorated, and so is the congregation. It is at times tense, at times relaxed. The way may be difficult and tortuous before becoming easy and straight leading to good organization.

I have found the Tao for living beings, but many profane people are still confused, attracted by honors, wealth, titles, and power and finally fall into abyss. Justice will determine their crimes, and you may predict the outcome.

If you understand the divine will, you should go straight to the end of your path.

All heart breaking changes in life are already arranged by divine will. In luck and misfortune of life, you should realize My existence and the Tao, and keep praying. All your worries would be recognized by Superior Spirits.

Understand!

Don't be disturbed and confused like ordinary people. Your mind would be bright, and able to prevent invasion of evils. All these words are from My loving heart and for you to remember. Otherwise, misery will come.

Understand!

Đ...., come to listen to My teachings and try to understand.

The human way is just like that!
You should always love living beings.
It's not easy to keep up with secular hardships.
You should often build up your credits by serving humanity.
Like the lonely crane contented at isolated place,
You should not return to the old friend waiting.

Don't try to reconnect the broken love,
But rather pay attention to the self cultivation in order to return to your position.

Your Karma debt has been fully paid, and the Tao would be a ladder for you to return to your original position. Understanding the divine will, understanding yourself, understanding living beings, are the ways to find the bright torch of the noble Tao in order to get out of the suffering ocean.

Ascension.

August 1, 1931 (Tân Mùi)
Here is Đại Đạo Tam Kỳ Phổ Độ Lý Giáo Tông.

Th…Tr…Nh…., I have given you one half of my authority, I just want to see whether you deserve it or not. I have dropped the responsibility of the 1st Governor of the three religions in exchange for the responsibility of Giáo Tông to create the stepping stones for all my younger brothers to reach their position.

Many times I have seen the difficulties in that responsibility, so I went ahead to stir up the situations so that evils would show up their true faces, and may be then eradicated by the Sacerdotal Council. I am watching your practice of justice in your three religions court. And I use the divine justice, giving many of you a chance to repent in the mercy of the Supreme Being. Otherwise, I have to excommunicate all of you. Don't think that the tumbling situation of the congregation could make me submit myself to you. This is my firm resolution. Try to fulfill your responsibility.

Ng…Tr…Th…, I congratulate you. The future of the Tao is in your hands. You should keep your authority. I am in You, and you are in me. My ability to move the divine mechanism depends on you. Try to follow the order. The Supreme Being is happy for you.

Th…T…Th…, I am happy for you. I promised to The Supreme Being to create a worthy position for you. You have to co-operate with me with all your sincerity

Now the administration is established, you should show your capability as the guardian of humanity. No emperor on earth could be compared to this divine position. Try to realize the importance if this responsibility in order to avoid evil seduction. Understand?

I have not seen anyone who builds up the name for the congregation with all his heart and mind. Instead, a lot of people are spoiling the congregation.

You should co-operate with me to fight them. Otherwise you could not avoid the fate that I have predicted. You have to get together with all great dignitaries of the Sacerdotal Council to eradicate evils. Otherwise, I would not promote any of you. You should understand that if you don't have enough majestic power, you could never win in this battle against evils. You took the responsibility to teach and train living beings about the Tao in order to save them. I will have ways to make evils show up their true faces. If you listen to their false words, you would become their arms to harm the Tao. Obey!

Ascension.

Thảo xá Hiền Cung Tây Ninh, December 23rd, 1931

YOUR MASTER, children

I am pleased to meet you all today.

Listen to this important recommendation to fulfill your duty assigned by Thái Bạch.

Remember there are two powers in the universe. Above is My supreme power, below is the power of living beings. I have created My visible body, which is the Sacerdotal Council of the great way, so I have to empower it so that it can save all living beings. You all belong to living beings and have also a power, the counterpart of mine. All living beings are My children, and may progress to the positions of Angels, Saints, Immortals, and Buddhas. There are many levels in the powers of living beings and human beings are the chief. I clearly said: "The supreme power is Mine, the living beings' power is My counterpart. Once those two powers become united, the tao would succeed reaching its true identity. I have granted the supreme power to the two leaders of the Sacerdotal Council, who are Giáo Tông and Hộ Pháp. Therefore, when the Giáo Tông and Hộ Pháp are united in one, this supreme power would become perfect. All living beings have their own power, My only counterpart.

Thái Bạch has been upset with you, because you did not obey the orders that he and the Hộ Pháp together have promulgated. From now on, any order from both of them should be considered by all living beings, Sacerdotal Council, and High Council, in order to study thoroughly and to implement.

Thái Bạch has promised to Me to promote more of you after the meeting of the three religions court of female dignitaries.

Try to obey him.
I bless all of you.

Ascension.

Pnom Penh Temple, the 4th day of the 2nd month of the year Nhâm Thân (March 20, 1932)

Here is Nguyệt Tâm Chơn Nhơn (Victor Hugo) Greetings to Quyền Giáo Tông, Hộ Pháp, Tiếp Đạo, and Overseas Mission.

Male and female dignitaries, listen.

Not many souls were found at the gate of Heaven, but a lot of them at the gate of Hell. I have never seen anyone who is not self respecting, useless to the universe, and who could reach the positions of Angels, Saints, Immortals, and Buddhas. The divine positions could never been reached by chance.

In obeying the order to be chief of the Overseas Mission, I follow the mercy of the Supreme Being, offer widely the religious way to all living beings, no matter their origin from primary or secondary or evil spirits, for them to use their credits of services to reach divine positions. They are all free to make decision to build up their credits of service depending on their situation. I just follow the law of justice, if they succeed, they will be accepted into their divine position, if not, they will be eliminated; I am tired to see impotent people.

I order you dignitaries to evaluate yourselves, and present all your crimes to Giáo Tông and Hộ Pháp for their future judgment.

Ascension.

Tay Ninh Holy See October 1932
THE EIGHTH LADY IMMORTAL OF THE JASPER POND PALACE
(Explanation on Âm Quang)

Âm Quang or Yin energy is the initial chaotic cosmic ether existing before the Supreme Being created the universe. This Yin energy is stored at the Diêu Trì Cung (Jasper Pond Palace) for the creation of the universe like the ovarian ova for the formation of human embryo. When the Supreme Being brings warm Yang energy, energy of life to interact with Yin energy to create the universe, the Yin energy becomes the center of creation and nurture of all beings. As the Yang energy expands, the Yin energy is pushed back and sunk down. Wherever the Yang energy has not reached, the Yin energy remained dark, indistinct, shadowy without life or incarnation and is therefore called Yin dimension, Hell, or dimension of sulfur. Many religions believe that it was the place for punishment of the souls with karmic attachments awaiting for reincarnation, but in reality, it is a dimension, a stopover between Hell and Nirvana, where souls stay to reflect on their past sins or good deeds before they are able to leave. The souls are afraid most of passing through this dimension. Thanks to this fear, any spiritual conscience remained in human body would help them to follow the Tao. Many souls have to stay at this dimension for hundreds of years depending on their purity level. The Supreme Being suggests vegetarian diet for humans to have enough purity to go through this dimension.

Honestly, if you are aware of it, you would be immensely terrified. If your soul is not pure you cannot return to the Supreme Being. I am aware of many souls who have to stay there for thousands of years. The 7th Lady Immortal has to stay there to support and guide them. All souls need help whether or not they are corrupted. Isn't it right?

Ascension.

Tây Ninh (Phạm Môn) February 12, 1933 (the 29th day of the 12th month of the year Quí Dậu)

Here is Bát Nương (the 8th female fairy)

How joyful to see us helping each other to succeed,
How joyful to see the Tao becoming beautiful and prosperous,
How joyful to know the physical body getting stronger,
How joyful for the conscience being more noble,
How joyful for human beings to have firm steps in the Tao,
How joyful for the blessed soul not being damaged,
How joyful for the Tao supporting the world,
How joyful for the right path becoming noble.

I am comfortable to witness the final arrangement of the Supreme Being. I remember when the Jade Palace determined the Hiệp Thiên Đài to hold the destiny of living beings and to establish the congregation, The Great Gentle Father changed the procedure and trusted that power to the Cửu Trùng Đài. All angels, Saints, Immortals, and Buddhas of the Jade Palace were surprised. The Great Gentle Father then taught: "Good! Not bad! You will understand My mind later."

Lục Nương Diêu Trì Cung (the sixth female fairy of the Jasper Pond Palace)

Greeting to all brothers!

I was at the Ngự Quan Cung, when the 8th female fairy announced that you were waiting, I hurried to come. This morning, I learned the good news: The Jade Court has changed the procedures. All divine records were destroyed, all rules were changed. Angels, Saints, Immortals, and Buddhas were happy. The Holy Mother of the Jasper Pond was extremely pleased so that she was shedding tears in giving this poem:

The children are still being breast fed,
Not being aware of their destiny,
Although the high power position of Ngự Mã is an honor,
But, may the destiny of the Hiệp Thiên be maintained.
The faded holy heart is challenged by secular seductions,
The bright body appearance would become wilted.
It's better to keep the same,
Because I am still worried, dear children!

Brother 2! That poem made every one of the Jasper Pond Palace shed tears. You should contemplate on it so that you won't get lost on your way to divine honor. Brothers Qu…, Th…, Kwan Yin ordered you to be patient and wait for her help.

Ascension.

The 17th day of the 3rd month of the year Quí Dậu (1933)

Here is Thường Cư Nam Hải Quan Âm Như Lai.

Greetings to all younger brothers and sisters.
Listen!
The most precious element of the Tao is harmony. Try to think. The creation of the universe is from the harmony between Yin and Yang energies. The creation and nurture of all living beings depend also on harmony. Even the organs inside of a person, need to have harmony to function, if not, human beings could not live. About the soul, if the six desires and the seven emotions rise against the conscience, and if they prevail, human beings would live solely according to the physical body needs, without realizing the divine will. What would be the value of such a person without harmony?

If there is no harmony in the family, there would be conflict between children and parents, separation between husband and wife, and between brothers and sisters.
If there is no harmony in a country, there would be turmoil. If there is no harmony in the world, humanity would fight each other. Therefore, I recommend you to create harmony first in any situation.

Ascension.

April 21, 1933 (year of Quí Dậu)

Here is Thường Cư Nam Hải Quan Âm Như Lai.

Greeting to all younger brothers and sisters.

Do you know why we have to love all living beings? Because the Mercy Father created all living beings in the universe, therefore they all have the same constituent. Therefore the love of life of the Great Mercy Father is unlimited. We are one of all species of the universe and are affected by the law of creation and nurture. If we kill one life, we would hurt the Great Mercy. When the Great Mercy hurts, so does the Heaven and the Earth. You think people would dare to hurt the Majesty?

Therefore, opening the heart to love all living beings including petty species is a way to avoid Karma law, because the divine law would never be partial to anyone. Even though we cannot see with our naked eyes, nothing could ever escape the divine law. The other reason is that when we are born in this earth, the Great Mercy has granted us a part of his spirit, which is more sacred than that granted to all other beings, so that we may replace God to guide all other weaker species. Try to think that in this world, would any father who happens to have a non pious child, not be sorrowful? And then, what happen if the Great Mercy Father has a child without universal love? Would human beings try to go against God, the Great Mercy Father?

Ascension.

May 8, 1933 (year Quí Dậu)

One cultivates sincere heart in a clear and just way,
The more one serves humanity, the more The Tao becomes bright.
With one gentle body, one may cultivate self
In order to reach enlightenment, and immortality.

Greetings to all younger brothers and sisters.
You have to participate often to worship ceremonies.
1- First, your soul would be brighter once it get closer to Superior Spirits,
2- Secondly, you may pray the Great Mercy to forgive you and all living beings,
3- Thirdly, when you perform rituals, you would have feelings and be receptive to the Great Mercy,
4- Fourthly, when you have feelings, you would open your loving heart and your conscience, and you become brighter.

Try to remember.

Regarding the spreading of the Tao, don't hurry too much, but also don't be lazy either.

Your sincerity would touch the Great Mercy, and your care would lead to success, even if it concerns petty matters. Moreover, the great Tao is extremely important for the saving of all living beings, who are floundered in the ocean of sufferings.

Try to follow my words so you may become glorious one day. This glory would never exist on earth.

Ascension.

Overseas Mission, Pnom Penh
The 3rd day of the 4th month of the year Quí Dậu (May 26, 1933)

Here is Nguyệt Tâm Chơn Nhơn or Victor Hugo.

Greetings to great dignitaries, friends, and younger sisters.

When the law is established, according to its use, it would need co-operation of people in order to create a great foundation with mutual love. The law has many aspects, which are applied according to different organizations. We may establish needed organizations and drop the unnecessary ones. The laws that the Supreme Being has created are useful for the executive organizations of the Great Way. If you follow the laws, the organization would succeed, if not, it would be destroyed. No exception for any member of the Sacerdotal Council. We have to follow His laws so that the Sacerdotal Council could acquire its authority. Anyone who acts against the laws, would cause turmoil.

Whoever acts against secular laws, would be judged by the society. Whoever acts against divine laws, would be excommunicated by the Sacerdotal Council, or be destroyed by divine power.

From now on, we should consider those people as enemies of the Sacerdotal Council, and should try to discard them. I have obeyed the order of the Jade Court to work for the Tao, I would not forgive them. From now on, The Overseas Mission will implement strictly the laws.
I pray to the Giáo Tông and Hộ Pháp to find ways to discard them without mercy.

Ascension.

The 9th day of the 4th month of the year Giáp Tuất (1934)

Here is the Seventh Female Fairy of the Jasper Pond Palace.

I regret that I have notified you the date I would come, but you didn't evoke me on time, so that I could not come to meet with you, and then some other places have used the name of the Jasper Pond Palace to cheat people. The damage is not negligible from the spiritual point of view. If we are dealing with evils, I would have ways to destroy them, but this matter was caused by the medium, I would have no ways to explain to superstitious people.

Dear sisters, I have to remind you that at the meeting at the Jade Court Palace regarding the reception of the laws from Nirvana, I overheard lamentation from The Địa Tạng Vương Bồ Tát (Ksitigarbha Bodhisattva) that he, as a Buddha, could not be able to get close to female souls to counsel them. Therefore, at the Yin dimension, there are more female than male who committed crimes. He wished to have a female fairy to take responsibility to teach female souls in order to save them from Yin dimension. I am very concerned and have already taken care of this issue. I am tired to see many souls suffering badly just for petty crimes. I have plans to help those souls avoid that Yin dimension.

First, I should explain the Yin dimension so that you may understand.

Yin dimension is the place that Theosophy calls waiting area for the souls who just passed away, or who are ready to re-incarnate. The Great Mercy Father has assigned that place as a meditation hall for the souls to contemplate on their good or bad deeds during their life. It is the place of self evaluation. If all living being know to self evaluate during their life, they would not have to stay at this Yin dimension. At the last resource, even if the souls have committed many crimes, and then may repent at the last minutes before their death and pray to the Supreme Being for forgiving and saving, they may receive blessing from Supreme Being and maybe able to avoid Yin dimension. This is the case when the souls repent, then receive and understand the teachings, they may save themselves, or may be saved thanks to their children's prayers.

Alas! Despite generous blessings from the Supreme Being, innumerable souls are still exiled to Yin dimension every day, because they didn't have enough faith in God, and violated their oath. I am so heart broken to see that most of them were female.

Ascension.

July 20, 1934

YOUR MASTER, children

......

Previously, the mediums were ignorant and did not have strong mind like you. In every séance, they were very tired after getting a few words from the spirit. If the mediums are totally unconscious, they may obtain excellent poems, but they may become confused afterward. By that way, there would be no way to spread the Tao.

(Question about the Superior Spirits entering the physical body of the mediums)

Your spirit is not comfortable in contact with evil energy. I use My energy to protect you and sometime have to enter you physical body. For the same reason, when you take the oath, My energy enters your body every time.

Here is your Master, children!

I congratulate you for your religious heart, My two children! Previously, I only ordered you to cure the diseases for the disciples, because I like to see your attitudes toward humanity. Your love toward humanity is very compatible with the love of life of the creator. Therefore, you have to care not only for disciples of other religions but also for your enemies.

Ascension.

The 15th day of the 7th month of the year Giáp Tuất (1934)

Here is Cao Thượng Phẩm.

…..

When I was still alive, I was so angry that I wished if I had my divine authority, I would fan them all away to Hell. But since I left my physical body and reached enlightenment, I became loving them so much that I was afraid that if they got lost in the wrong path, I would lose a precious spiritual friend. Therefore, I have to guide them for each of their steps, depending on the level of their mind and heart. If by chance, I failed to guide them back to their original position, I would try at least to prevent their exile to Hell, by praying to the three religions court to allow them to re-incarnate to pay off their karma debt.

Dear brother! Would you be satisfied to watch the congregation tumbled down just because of petty meaningless matters?

Responsibility is the primary importance. Personal matters are secondary. You should realize your origin in order to avoid routine mistakes. Superior Spirits have often said: "Secular honors and wealth are petty matters, the fame of the Tao is more important. Treat people equally regardless their names, even if you have to sacrifice your personal interest in order to fulfill your duty." The progress of the Tao has been very delayed. It's a kind of wasting all the hardship of the Master to found the Tao for us to save living beings. The delay is due to the people's profane heart. Please don't blame anyone. Don't make anyone suffer. Life is an ocean of sufferings, and a shore of confusion. If one may escape from that suffering ocean, one wouldn't like to waste their life to be confused and lost in the midst of secular attractions.

Ascension.

The 16th day of the 7th month of the year Giáp Tuất (1934)

Here is Thái Thượng Đạo Tổ.

Greeting to all disciples.
Smile. Perhaps you all are surprised for my sudden unexpected visit!
(M...Ng...replied: Yes Sir, indeed we are, because Thượng Phẩm has announced the coming of the Supreme Being)
The Supreme being trusted me to reveal some secret indispensable matters to guide you through this turmoil of the congregation.
M..Ng…! Do you remember my previous explanation using different ways and terms to guide you?
Divine mechanism is miraculous to humanity. But to the Tao, it is even more miraculous and more important so that even intelligent people couldn't understand it thoroughly. The many roles that the Supreme Being has arranged on the stage of the Tao are not different from the roles of ancient prophets responsible to guide humanity in the old times. If you like to be calm, to suppress you internal fire, you have to have immense energy, and a generous heart so that you would not be angry toward many disciples who, by following the divine orders, have created turmoil in this furtive heavy world. You should understand that every thing that happens has a term and a cause. You and even your elders should evaluate the situation based on the virtues of people. You may then understand the colossal miraculous arrangements of the Supreme Being.

In the old times, Hớn Bái Công was not a clear sighted king, but the divine mechanism had arranged his dynasty to last three hundred years. He was jealous with talented persons, he was not trustful, kept listening to inquisitive words and kill useful meritorious people. Anyone other than Trương Lương would get angry and complain. Lots of other foolish kings such as excessively lustful Võ Tắc Thiên, extremely non virtuous Tùy Dương Đế, tyrannical Sở Hạng, debauched
Tần Thủy Hoàng, were also arranged by the divine mechanism to stay on their throne for a long time, despite their unjust actions against many meritorious officials!

Smile! That was about secular life. It is the same in the religious life. Every thing happens according to divine laws. The heroes with heavy responsibility to the country would have to fulfill their duty, and their merits would be reported to the divine court or recorded in history but not to those foolish leaders.

Alas! The anger usually destroys all great works of the past.
You just pay attention to actions of others, but know nothing about divine will of the Supreme Being. You are aware of the situation, but don't set time to create opportunities to guide living beings on time.

I ask you four friends, among you, who has ever suffered in life for the happiness of living beings?

(T... Đ... answered)

Smile! That is nothing compared to virtuous people of the old times. If the Supreme Being did not found the Tao early, I am afraid that 20 to 30 years later, all current primary souls would have to re-incarnate many times. Time has passed away quickly. Living beings are getting lost, confused, without having any shining wisdom torch. M...Ng..., do you know how would be the end?

Probably not! But because of your divine position, please pay attention to living beings. Would you agree?

(M...Ng... responded)

Smile! Responsibility is responsibility. If you like to work, any work would not be enough, any time wouldn't be early. When you think that it's early, that is because your mind hasn't been set. The Supreme Being has modified the way just because of the love for His children. Couldn't you change your mind to become more generous, to deserve that love?

Evils? Just? Smile! Even myself, I could not determine whether it's right or wrong. No body could predict the chance. In misfortune, there may always be luck and vice versa. It's difficult to predict. Just do what is needed to be done. Talking about right or wrong, no one in this world with the physical body could say that he/she is right. Many evil events happen with a cause. That is the case of evils used by the divine will, by the three religions court to challenge people, or by demons to disturb the Tao. They all lead to divine results. At the end, you just need to return to the Master with your sincere heart and all the services you have done to humanity.

The congregation was divided into three. M...Ng..., where do you like to serve? Holy See, the center, or the delta?

(M...Ng...: at the Holy See)

Holy See is the root of the Tao. If you like to serve there, according to the instruction of the Master, you can go ahead. You may change your way of practice depending on the situation, according to your own responsibility, and I don't want to interfere with your decision.

If you hesitate, it would be too late. You should evaluate yourself. Secular life is different from religious life. You should recognize your mistakes that have caused sufferings to yourself.

Ascension.

Hộ Pháp Residence, the 18th day of the 10th month of the year Ất Hợi (November 13, 1935)

Here is Lý Thái Bạch.
Greetings to Hộ Pháp, dignitaries of Hiệp Thiên Đài, Cửu Trùng Đài and Overseas Mission.

Wait for the Thượng Phẩm to release the corbeille a bec.

I come to the private residence of the Hộ Pháp, so I excuse the rituals. You may all stand up. Hộ Pháp, because there was no séance set up, I could not come to chat with you. Secondly, because the divine mechanism has changed, it's useless for me to come. Today because of the enthronement ceremony, I like to come here to congratulate you all. I like to thank Hộ Pháp for his patience and hardship in improving the congregation. I am ashamed for not helping. Thanks.

(Hộ Pháp addressed: ......)

Smile! Needless to say, you would see clearly that even if I like to do anything, my hands would be tightly tied in front of a powerless Sacerdotal Council. What a luck! The divine mechanism has not been corrupted, so now I have a chance to execute my power.

(Hộ Pháp addressed: The divine mechanism has changed, I would like to return to you the responsibility of Giáo Tông, so that you may be fully empowered to handle the divine arrangement).

Smile! I am afraid that it isn't so. Firstly, since I have given it away, I would not take it back. Secondly, it's easy to administer, but difficult to discipline. If you don't have the half of my power, you would not be able to run the Sacerdotal Council. So leave it as it is for now.

Listen to this poem and try to understand:

From now on, the saving boat is stable,
To run forward in the suffering ocean to save living beings.
With full miraculous instinct, you may row away from sufferings,
Enough miracles would help to neutralize Karma.
I will be responsible for empowering the boat,
All Superior Spirits will comfort you.
You have surmounted many storms many times,
You may close the Hell with your evils fighting staff.

Ascension.

INDEX

Allan Kardec 86
An Hoa, name of a city 130
An, name of a person 54
Angkor Thom 162
Angkor Wat 162
Automatic writing 25
B., name of a person 250
Bach Ngoc Chung Dai, Tower for the White Pearl Bell 191
Bach Ngoc Chung, White Pearl Bell 50
Bach Ngoc Kinh, White Pearl Palace, Jade Palace, Jade Court Palace 28, 55, 69, 70, 77, 80, 112, 118, 138, 265, 271
Ban, name of a person 51, 70, 137, 138
Bao 145
Bao Dao 145, 242
Bao Phap 144
Bao The 145
Bat Nha boat 129, 184
Bat Quai Dai, Octagonal Palace 191
Bich, name of a person 54
Binh Thanh, baptismal name of Mr. Binh 191
Binh, name of a person 73, 137
Bo Tat, Boddhisattva 72
Brahma 95
Buddhahood 57
Buddhist canon 46
C..., name of a person 178, 211, 215, 216, 219, 225
Ca Na pond 191, 192
Ca, name of a person 170
Can Giuoc, name of a city 46, 56, 65
Cao Duc Trong, name of a person 145
Cao Thuong Pham, baptismal name of Mr. Cao Quynh Cu 161, 274
Cau Kho, name of a city 134, 146, 148, 205, 229

Cau Nhiem, name of a city 232
CH., name of a person 182, 218, 225
Chanh Phoi Su 97
Character Tam 50
Chau Cong 95
Chau Dynasty, a Dynasty of China 58
Chieu, name of a person 24, 43
Cho Dem, name of a city 147
Cholon, name of a city 67, 89, 117, 119, 139, 204, 230
Chon Cuc Lao Su 228
Christ 102, 103, 110, 111
Christianity 79, 154, 167
Chuong Phap, Censor Cardinal 73, 96, 97, 98, 123, 136, 138
Chuong, name of a person 51
Compassionate Master 153, 156
Concordance 28, 228
Confucianism 147
Confucius 80, 245
Cong, Dung, Ngon, Hanh 130
Conscience 112, 119, 129, 140, 240, 244, 265, 267, 269
Cosmic Ether 59, 83
Cu, name of a person 24, 38, 42, 46, 50, 54, 65, 72, 136
Cuu Thien Cam Ung Loi Thinh Pho Hoa Thien Ton 38
Cuu Trung Dai 227, 265, 278
D. Q., name of a person 89
D., name of a person 69, 92, 110, 111, 223, 257, 276
Daemon 112
Dai Dan, name of a séance 89, 117, 119, 148
Dao Ngu Cung pieces 50
Dao Quang, name of a person 84
Dao, Tao 31
Dau Su, Cardinal 37, 38, 46, 56, 73, 96, 97, 98, 123, 138, 203, 217
Demonic Spirit 29
Demons 64, 65, 69, 75, 113, 114, 154, 155, 277
Dia Tang Vuong Bo Tat, Ksitigarbha Bodhisattva 271
Dieu Tri Cung, Jasper Pond Palace 264

Disasters from East to West 172, 178, 189, 251
Divine Eye 32, 73, 82, 214
Divine Light 42
Divine mechanism 100, 117, 129, 140, 151, 249, 259, 275
Duc, name of a person 24, 39, 42, 50, 70, 144
Duong, name of a person 55, 123, 138, 170
Eighth female fairy, eighth lady immortal, Bat Nuong 163, 264, 265, 266
Elias, Elijah 86, 95
Eternity 194, 245
Evils 64
Falsehood 34
Female College 92, 93, 94, 137, 138
Final judgment 119
Five Branches of the Great Way 41
Five Thunder Lords 39
Flammarion 86
French citizens 49
G..., name of a person 45, 78, 79
Gia Dinh, name of a city 139
Giac Hai pagoda 167
Giang Ma Xu 39, 66
Giang, name of a person 24, 40
Giao Huu 41, 97, 137, 138, 150, 205
Giao Su 42, 97, 137, 138, 170
Giao Tong, Pope 38, 73, 96, 97, 98, 144, 212, 217, 255, 259, 261, 263, 270
Gioi, name of a person 51
Giong Ong To, name of a city 61
Go Ken, name of a city 159, 160, 191
H., name of a person 185, 195, 204, 225, 247
Hai Phong, name of a city 139
Han Dynasty, Hon Dynasty, a Dynasty of China 58, 67, 166, 174
Han Tin, name of a person 196
Hang Trong Son, name of a person 166
Hanoi, name of a city 139

Harmony 186, 224, 232, 233, 267
Hau, name of a person 24, 39, 42, 50, 65, 106, 144
Heaven 156, 263, 268
Hell 41, 67, 69, 91, 154, 263, 264, 274, 279
Hien 145
Hien Dao 145
Hien Phap 144
Hien The 145
Hien Vien Huynh De Dynasty, a Dynasty of China 58
Hiep Ninh, name of a city 142
Hiep Thien Dai, Heavenly Union Palace 96, 97, 123, 144, 145, 191, 203, 204, 211, 219, 220, 226, 227, 265, 266, 278
Hierarchical Council 201
Hierarchy 70
Hieu, name of a woman 51, 72, 136
Ho Phap 40, 66, 96, 97, 123, 126, 144, 191, 217, 238, 261, 263, 270, 278
Ho Quang Chau, name of a person 84
Hoa, name of a person 106
Hoai, name of a person 24, 43
Hoang, name of a person 54
Hoc, name of a person 71
Hoi Phuoc Tu, Hoi Phuoc temple 46
Holy Doctrine 41
Holy See 143, 155, 191, 213, 218, 224, 225, 232, 242, 246, 254, 277
Hon Bai Cong, name of a person 275
Hon Luu Bang, name of a person 214
Hong Quan Lao To 95
HTD, name of a person 208
Hu Vo, Cosmic Void 66
Hue Mang Kim Tien, name of an Immortal 68
Hue, name of a city 139
Huon, name of a person 24
Huong, name of a person 71, 138
Huynh Kim Khuyet 118
Isrealites 110, 111

Jade Emperor Temple 44
Jasper Pond Palace, Dieu Tri Cung 264, 266, 271
Jehovah of the Hebrews 110, 111
Jeremiah 95
Jesus, Jesus Christ 80, 86, 95
Jews 110, 111
John the Baptist 95
Judgment day 187, 189
K…, name of a person 53, 60, 95, 198
Karma 75, 103, 140, 147, 151, 189, 195, 196, 200, 246, 258, 268, 274, 279
Karmic law 46
Karmic wheel 133
Kha, name of a person 92
Khai 145
Khai Dao 145
Khai Phap 144
Khai The 145
Khi 32, 56, 61, 83, 126, 127, 237, 238, 239
Kiet, name of a person 73
Kim Quang Tien charm 38, 66
Kim, name of a person 51, 66
Kinh Thanh, baptismal name of Mr. Kinh 70
Kinh, name of a person 51, 70
Ky Thanh, baptismal name of Mr. Ky 70
Ky, name of a person 24, 42, 43, 51, 70
L…, name of a person 60, 102, 103, 205, 206, 211, 219
Lake Dong Dinh, Dong Dinh lake 184, 192
Lam Huong Thanh, name of a person 138, 186
Lam, name of a person 167, 170
Lao Tse 35, 58, 80, 95
Le Sanh 67, 98, 138
Le Son, name of a saint 92, 93
Lecturer Taoist 42
Lich, Le Van Lich, name of a person 36, 37, 39, 42, 45, 50, 54, 67, 70, 75
Loi Am Co Dai, tower for the Thunder Drum 191

Loi Am Tu, Thunderous Temple 68, 69
Long Thanh, name of a city 142
Luat, name of a person 123, 138
Luc Nuong, sixth lady immortal, sixth female fairy 266
Luc To 46
Lucifer 154
Luu Khoan, name of a person 166
Luu, name of a person 72
Ly Bach, Ly Thai Bach, Thai Bach 38, 66, 67, 89, 90, 104, 108, 109, 118, 124, 134, 137, 138, 139, 143, 151, 153, 155, 156, 160, 187, 191, 193, 203, 205, 206, 217, 231, 242, 247, 250, 254, 261, 262, 278
M., name of a French person 88, 92, 108, 109, 166, 196, 223, 228, 229, 242, 244, 246, 275, 276
Major ceremony 31
Man, name of a person 24
Manh, name of a person 145
Matthew 122
Medium 25
Minh Duong sect, a Taoist sect 51
Minh Ly Dan, name of a cenacle 158
Minh Tan, name of a Taoist sect 92, 93, 94
Minh, name of a person 24, 51, 70
Moses 86
Mother Goddess 164
Mount Sinai 86
Muoi, name of a person 51, 94
N., name of a person 166, 184, 196, 211, 223, 228, 229, 246
Nam Xuan pieces 50
New Codes 50, 74, 82, 84, 118, 123, 138, 201, 215, 227
Ng. Tr. Th., baptismal name of a person 259
Ng., name of a person 169, 242, 244, 275, 276
Nghia, name of a person 50, 65, 70, 144
Nghiet Canh Dai 61, 62, 132, 237
Ngoc Co, basket with beak 138
Ngoc Dan, name of a séance 53, 56, 61
Ngoc Hoang Sam drum 50

Ngoc Hu Cung, Ngoc Hu Palace, Invisible Jade Palace 46, 68, 220, 240
Ngoc Lich Nguyet, religious name of Mr. Lich 39, 217
Ngoc Tam, name of a person 92
Ngoc Y, name of a person 92
Ngu Ma, a celestial title 266
Ngu Quan Cung, name of a palace 266
Nguon Thi 80, 95, 167
Nguyet Tam Chon Nhon, religious name of saint Victor Hugo 263, 270
Nhan Am Dao Truong, name of a Taoist 214, 247, 253
Nhien Dang Co Phat, Dipankara Buddha 35, 58, 95
Nhon, name of a person 50
Nhu Nhan, name of a Buddhist monk 167
Nirvana 25, 28, 41, 45, 83, 95, 103, 112, 113, 114, 132, 133, 140, 159, 169, 171, 175, 181, 185, 201, 202, 209, 229, 244, 247, 264, 271
North Star 73
Nothingness 162
Nuong, name of a person 123, 138
O Mon, name of a city 95
Oath 39, 40, 70, 84, 93, 94, 272, 273
Perfume river 185
Peter 80
Pham Mon, name of an organization 265
Pham Tang, name of a person 196
Phan Thi Lan, name of a woman 84
Phap, Dharma 82
Pho Giao Su 170
Phoi Su, 97, 123, 137, 138, 163
Phu Nhuan, name of a city 152
Phu, name of a person 72
Phuoc Long, name of a city 147
Phuoc, name of a person 145
Phuong Thien Mao 138
Pnom Penh 250, 263, 270
Precepts 158

Prostration 32
Qu., name of a person 266
Quan Am Bo Tat, Quan Am Bodhisattva, Quan Yin, Kwan Yin, Guan Yin Ru Lai 43, 58, 65, 66, 67, 89, 142, 151, 170, 186, 187, 197, 206, 266
Quan Thanh De Quan, Kuan Kung, Guan Gong, Guan Sheng Di Jun 43, 65, 66, 67, 89, 187, 251
Qui, name of a person 24
Reincarnation 130, 140, 147, 161, 169, 176, 177, 178, 181, 209
S., name of a person 196, 219
Sacerdotal Council 138, 143, 150, 154, 203, 205, 259, 260, 270, 278
Saigon, name of Vietnam's capital 139, 161, 165
Sakya Muni 35, 36, 46, 58, 80, 82, 95, 167, 191, 223, 248
Sang, name of a person 24, 50, 65, 72
Sanh, name of a person 24, 43
Satan 58, 219, 243
Science 79
Second body 25
Seventh lady immortal 264, 271
So Dynasty 232
So Hang, name of a person 275
Spiritism 25
St. Peter gate 132
T..., name of a person 60, 90, 134, 157, 172, 173, 195, 196, 215, 216, 219, 221, 225, 242, 243, 276
Ta, name of a person 71
Tac 24, 38, 46, 50, 54, 65, 72, 136
Tam Ky Pho Do 36
Tan Dynasty 232
Tan mountain 180
Tan Thuy Hoang, name of a person 275
Tang, humanity 82
Taoism 167
Tay ninh 104, 123, 126, 136, 139, 159, 170, 186, 191, 224, 242, 244, 261, 265

Te Thien Dai Thanh 92
Th. T. Th., baptismal name of a person 259
Th..., name of a person 162, 175, 180, 184, 205, 206, 232, 242, 266
Thai At, name of an immortal 158
Thai Nuong Tinh, baptismal name of Mr. Nuong 217
Thai Tho, baptismal name of Mr, Tho 160
Thai Thuong Nguon Thi, Thai Thuong Lao Quan, Thai Thuong Dao To 35, 66, 92, 275
Than 32, 56, 83, 126, 238
Than Hoang Bon Canh 126
Than Tu 46, 47
Thanh Dao 66
Thanh, baptismal name 66
Thao Xa Hien Cung, name of a place 261
Thau, name of a person 145
Third Salvation, Third Universal Salvation 92, 93, 94, 99, 117, 129, 130, 162, 169, 171, 172, 177, 178, 212, 219
Tho Thanh, Thai Tho Thanh, baptismal name of Mr. Tho 104, 123, 138
Tho, name of a person 65, 66, 73, 106, 123, 137, 138
Thong Thien Giao Chu 95
Three offerings 31
Thuong Cu Nam Hai Quan Am Nhu Lai, name of Quan Yin Boddhisattva 267, 268
Thuong Dynasty, a Dynasty of China 58
Thuong Pham 123, 144, 145, 191, 216, 242
Thuong Sanh 123, 144, 145, 216
Thuong Trung Nhut, Th. Tr. Nh., baptismal name of Mr. Trung 39, 125, 160, 203, 217, 259
Thuong Tuong Thanh, baptismal name of Mr. Tuong
Thuong, name of a person 66
Tien Dao Cong Than 42
Tien Dao Medium Assistant Taoist 42
Tien Hac Medium Assistant Taoist 42
Tien Ong, Immortal 72
Tien Sac Lang Quan 42

Tiep 145
Tiep Dao 145, 263
Tiep Phap 144
Tiep The 145
Tiep, name of a person 51
Tieu Son Taoist 226
Tinh 32, 56, 61, 83, 126, 237, 238
Tr…, name of a person 60, 162, 172, 180, 186, 190, 195, 201, 202, 204, 205, 206, 208, 210, 231, 232, 246, 249, 254, 257
Trang Thanh, baptismal name of Mr. Trang 70
Trang, name of a person 50, 65, 70, 71, 90, 106, 144
Tri, name of a person 54
Trinh, name of a person 136
Triune-faith court, Triune-faith convention, Triune-religion court, Three Religions Court 106, 117, 146, 151, 184, 210, 216, 219, 259, 274
Tro, name of a person 137, 138
Trung, Le Van Trung 36, 37, 38, 42, 43, 51, 70, 75, 84, 90, 106, 116, 136, 150, 153, 158
Truoc, name of a person 71
Truong Luong, name of a person 275
Truong Tu Phong 196
Truong, name of a person 174
Tu Hang Dao Nhan, Tu Hang Master 58
Tu Lam, name of a temple 96, 99, 170
Tu, self-improvement 116
Tuoi, name of a person 51
Tuong, name of a person 51, 65, 67, 71, 90, 106, 130, 136
Tuy Duong De, name of a person 275
Ty, name of a person 51
Universal Congress 109
Universal globe 191
Universal truth 25
Ursa Major 73
Ursa Minor 73
V., name of a French person 88, 92

Van Phap 229
Van Xuong, title of a angel 143
Van, name of a person 51, 93
Vegetarianism 25, 56
Vi river 180
Vi, name of a person 92, 93
Victor Hugo 263, 270
Vinh Nguyen Tu, Vinh Nguyen temple 35, 50
Vinh, name of a person 145
Vo Tac Thien, name of a person 275
Vo Uu shoes 138
Way of Angels 41
Way of Buddhas 41
Way of humanity 41
Way of Immortals 41
Way of Saints 41
White Pearl Gate 53
White Pearl Palace, White Jade Palace 77, 80, 95, 209
Yang 31, 234, 264, 267
Yin, Am Quang 31, 234, 264, 267, 271, 272
Zodiacal dignitaries 123, 144, 145
Zodiacs 32

Contact information:

Hum D. Bui, MD.
Phone: (909) 534-0145
Email: hongbui24568@gmail.com

CPSIA information can be obtained
at www.ICGtesting.com
Printed in the USA
LVHW040800080122
708038LV00014B/53